"In *Seven Steps to Your Best Life* [...] iently shares his powerful *Stage Climbing* strategies to reach the highest potential in every area of your life. An easy and simple guide to fulfillment."

—Deepak Chopra, *New York Times* bestselling author of *The Healing Self: A Revolutionary New Plan to Supercharge Your Immunity and Stay Well for Life*

"*Seven Steps to Your Best Life* will introduce many to the Stage Climbing process, a highly effective series of strategies for living life at your highest potential. Dr. Broder shows how to maximize your unique passions and purpose by systematically clearing away blockages that obstruct your access to that zone within you. I recommend this book to people who desire to manifest their greatest dreams."

—John Perkins, *New York Times* bestselling author of *The New Confessions of an Economic Hit Man* and *Hoodwinked*

"This fast-moving, enjoyable book shows you how to perform and achieve at your best in every area of your life. Get more done, make more money and succeed faster than you every thought possible."

—Brian Tracy, speaker, consultant, and author of *Maximum Achievement*

"It is time to release *your full potential in all your dimensions* and this book will inspire you to your highest stage!! Happy Reading!"
—Mark Victor Hansen,
Cocreator of the #1 *New York Times*
bestselling series *Chicken Soup for the Soul*

"I highly recommend *Seven Steps to Your Best Life* for anyone who would like to understand, accept, or change an aspect of his or her life. Dr. Broder offers a brand-new approach that will get you the results you want for your career, relationships, spirituality, or any part of your life where you apply it."
—Peggy McColl, *New York Times*
bestselling author of *Your Destiny Switch*

"*Seven Steps to Your Best Life: The Stage Climbing Solution for Living the Life You Were Born to Live* contains one of the most innovative and brilliant models for helping people to change at the deepest levels. *I have successfully used it on myself* as well as with the clients I counsel, and strongly recommend it to anyone seriously seeking to gain a better understanding of themselves and take control of their lives very quickly."
—Karyne B. Wilner, Psy.D., clinical psychologist and
director, Professional Program in Core Living Therapy

"With precision, clarity, wisdom and heart; in *Seven Steps to Your Best Life*, Michael Broder takes you through the process of *Stage Climbing* towards the task of greater knowledge and awareness about one's highest potential. This is magical."

—Murray Needleman, Ph.D.,
clinical and media psychologist

"Dr. Broder has distilled a lifetime of professional service into a unique set of perspectives . . . and a set of highly effective strategies for transforming this clarity into meaningful change within our everyday lives. With practical guidelines for enhancing parenting, career selection, and love relationships; *Seven Steps to Your Best Life* is a "must read" for human service professionals, as well as anyone seeking a wonderful 'road map' for more successful living."

—Bruce Coopersmith, Ph.D.,
clinical psychologist and
author of *Buying Without Regrets*

"*Seven Steps to Your Best Life* introduces a new, simple, yet powerful tool. It cuts to the chase in helping you understand your life as well as taking it to the next level with the many effective strategies offered. I highly recommend it to anyone who wants to see immediate results!"

—Fran Grabosky, psychologist, Tampa, Florida

"If we're fortunate, our lives will be touched by a person, a process, or an insight that resonates so deeply in our soul that we feel we've brushed up against an absolute truth. Dr. Michael Broder's *Seven Steps to Your Best Life: The Stage Climbing Solution for Living the Life You Were Born to Live* hits that mark as he describes the process, in great detail, for us to shake off all of the things that stop us from reaching our potential. In our work at CoupleWise we aim to provide the tools to help you have the best relationship or marriage possible. We look forward to integrating Dr. Broder's approaches into future versions of our CoupleWise program.
—Dan Gallo and Dr. Gary Krane,
Founder of CoupleWise

"*Seven Steps to Your Best Life: The Stage Climbing Solution for Living the Life You Were Born to Live* offers a masterful integration of cognitive therapy tools across the developmental life span. It encourages self-acceptance and honest self-assessment. With amazing detail, Dr. Broder prescribes activities and tools to cognitively dispute limiting beliefs at each stage, leading the reader to pursue desired incremental behavioral changes towards living life at one's fullest potential."
—Barbara Lyn Grinnell, Ph.D., licensed psychologist

"Michael Broder's *Seven Steps to Your Best Life* is a thoughtful, manageable, and elegant approach to our important therapeutic work. It provides a brilliantly useful and succinct paradigm for understanding and promoting clients' resources, development, and growth . . . Michael, you did it again!"

—Elaine R. Axelrod, PhD.,
Psychologist and shamanic practitioner

"Michael Broder brings self-actualizing theory into the twenty-first century. He presents an optimistic vision of how through self-reflection of one's development in different stages of life, one can create the motivation and self-efficacy needed for change and development of one's full potential."

—Michael E. Bernard, Ph.D.,
professor, Melbourne Graduate School of Education,
University of Melbourne; founder, You Can Do It! Education

"I fully recommend *Seven Steps to Your Best Life: The Stage Climbing Solution for Living the Life You Were Born to Live*, by Dr. Michael Broder. He has a special way of engaging and his compassion shines through. If you follow his ideas you will ascend to good mental health."

—Windy Dryden, Ph.D.,
professor of psychotherapeutic studies,
Goldsmiths, University of London
and author or editor of over 200 books

"The concepts in *Seven Steps to Your Best Life: The Stage Climbing Solution for Living the Life You Were Born to Live* integrate a variety of developmental and therapeutic psychological theories in a well-organized and practical manner that is useful to practitioners and laypeople alike. When looking at careers, romantic relationships, family relationships, altruistic endeavors, and other facets of life, I thought of scenarios in my own life, the lives of friends and loved ones, and my patients. Personally, the concepts gave me courage to enact behavior change by addressing a professional issue with an authority figure; I felt empowered for having stood up for myself! I have no doubt this approach would be useful for helping many with understanding and changing their own behavior by realizing the areas in their own life that could benefit from growth and change."

—Alicia T. Rozycki Lozano, Ph.D.,
psychologist, Jacksonville, FL

"*Seven Steps to Your Best Life* is so illuminating. It has helped me understand not only when I developed certain behaviors but also why and what needs each one was originally intended to address, and this insight has increased my acceptance of myself and others and provided me with a path to greater purpose and meaning in my life."

—Carol Noblitt, director of development,
Getting Out and Staying Out

"Dr. Broder has developed an important and thoughtful approach, one which is indispensable to mental-health professionals but also accessible to anyone valuing psychological well-being. Although based on complex psychological theories and on the shoulders of such greats as Maslow and Erickson, Dr. Broder has created a simple system to facilitate psychological growth and enable you to be more impactful in your life. He has formulated a well-organized, clear, concise method for exploring deep psychological processes. In that process, he has revealed himself to be an important theorist in the field of psychology. What also comes through is Dr. Broder's respect and passion for his profession and its powerful potential not only to heal, but to enable one to live a more fulfilling and meaningful life."

—Dr. Marion Rudin Frank,
president, Professional Psychology Services;
founder, Philadelphia Jungian Professional Club;
licensed senior psychologist

"Michael Broder has done it again! His innovative way of categorizing behavior according to a person's level of maturity helps my clients to move towards their goals in the most efficient manner."

—Jacqueline Summers, licensed psychologist

"*Seven Steps to Your Best Life* represents a breakthrough. It is a completely new career and personal development tool that takes a jumble of feelings and descriptions and drills them down into discreet categories that anyone can understand. It concisely let me see where I was in my career and personal development and it gave me the tools I needed to achieve greater development and more fulfillment."

—Sharon P. Stein, health-care and medical-sales professional representing top ten pharmaceutical firms as well as the American Red Cross

"*Stage Climbing* provides me with an intelligent framework for organizing my thoughts and deciding the most efficient place to intervene when I'm working with a client."

—Arlene Foreman, licensed professional counselor, A Center for Marriage Counseling

"*Seven Steps to Your Best Life* is such a wonderfully helpful guide to getting the most out of life and bettering ourselves along the way."

—B.J. Rosenfeld, author of *The Chameleon in the Closet*

Seven Steps
to Your
Best Life

Seven Steps to Your Best Life

The Stage Climbing Solution for Living the Life You Were Born to Live

Michael S. Broder, Ph.D.

MEDIA

Published 2019 by Gildan Media LLC
aka G&D Media.
www.GandDmedia.com

First Edition: 2019

Front Cover design by David Rheinhardt of Pyrographx

Interior design by Meghan Day Healey of Story Horse, LLC.

Library of Congress Cataloging-in-Publication Data is available upon request

ISBN: 978-1-7225-1013-8

Manufactured in the United States of America by LSC Communications

10 9 8 7 6 5 4 3 2 1

*To my wife Arlene, my daughter Joanne,
and my amazing grandsons, Adam and Kyle*

Contents

CHAPTER FOUR

Stage Two
Taming Your Primitive Self   35

CHAPTER FIVE

Stage Three
Living Life by Your Rules   57

CHAPTER SIX

Stage Four
Becoming Fearless   81

CHAPTER SEVEN

Stage Five
Taking Charge of Your Life   105

CHAPTER EIGHT

Stage Six
Follow Your Passion   133

CHAPTER NINE

Stage Seven
When Benevolence Takes Over   175

CHAPTER TEN

Calibrating Your Stage Climb
The Shortest Path from Where You Are Now
to Where You Want to Be   199

Contents

Acknowledgments

Seven Steps to Your Best Life: The Stage Climbing Solution for Living the Life You Were Born to Live is a user-friendly version of Stage Climbing, an original concept and highly effective approach that powers the bulk of the strategies I present in this book. It is also a result of the inspiration, collaboration, influence, and guidance of many incredible people, whom I am grateful to have had around me throughout my career.

I heartily thank my agent and friend, Dan Strutzel, for believing in the Stage Climbing concept as a powerful mechanism of change and for his commitment to bringing it to as many people as possible. Dan connected me with an amazing team at G&D to make this happen, beginning with Gilles E. Dana, publisher, and Ellen Goldberg, managing editor. I am very indebted to two extraordinary publishing professionals for their hands-on contribution to this work: our editor, Richard Smoley, and designer, Meghan Day Healey.

The two psychologist colleagues I am most proud of for their ongoing support, wisdom, and help in creating the Stage Climbing concept: My wife and colleague, Dr. Arlene Goldman, is a psychologist who believed in Stage Climbing from the very beginning and has been involved in every aspect of bringing this book to fruition. She continues to be an invaluable resource for helping to shape the Stage Climbing vision and expanding its applications. My daughter, Dr. Joanne Broder, a highly accomplished research psychologist, was not only of tremendous help with some of the technical aspects of Stage Climbing, but actually began being a resource for it the day she was born. Joanne, this book contains many of the principles by which I raised you, and it's been an added joy to observe you as a parent to our beloved grandsons, Adam and Kyle.

Throughout my entire professional life, I have been blessed with having world class mentors who helped shape my thinking. They include: Dr. William Swartley, a pioneer of the human potential movement in the 1970s. Bill was an early mentor who first helped me make what was at the time a counterintuitive connection between human development, cognition, psychodynamics, and personal growth. In addition, three of my mentors happen to be men who are recognized as the three most influential icons of the cognitive behavior therapy orientation—Drs. Albert Ellis (REBT), Arnold Lazarus (Multimodal Therapy) and Aaron T. Beck (CBT)—which is the principal foundation for Stage Climbing. Working with these giants as well as with many others far too numerous to mention has always been my inspiration for thinking outside of the box.

My gratitude goes out to colleagues and members of my team who made important contributions to various aspects of Stage Climbing and this project. They include Jacques Bazinet, Dr. Michael Bernard, Dr. Bruce Coopersmith, Dr. Sari Fleischman, Fran Grabosky, Dr. Barbara Grinnell, Dave Kuenstle, Dr. Murray Needleman, Sam Simpson, and Jackie Snyder. In addition, John Perkins, *New York Times* bestselling author, mentor, and friend, provided me invaluable help in making the Stage Climbing approach a tool that virtually anyone can use to achieve rapid and lasting results in their lives. Thank you all for your invaluable input!

Finally, let me express my everlasting gratitude to the many thousands of clients I've seen in psychotherapy and that I have coached (some of whom have shared their stories for this book); the many thousands more mental-health professionals I've trained; and the millions I've reached through my talks, radio shows, audio programs, previous books and articles, TV and other media appearances throughout my career spanning over four decades. I have learned something from every one of you that hopefully has found its way into these pages!

To the Reader
Your Highest Potential Awaits You!

*What lies before us and what lies behind us
are tiny matters compared to what lies within us.*
—Ralph Waldo Emerson

Welcome to what I hope for you is a life-changing journey! It's a journey designed to put at your disposal all the tools you need to reach a very special destination: your best life, that is, *your highest potential*—the zone where you are fully connected to and living by *your unique passions and purpose*—in virtually any and every area of your life.

Here's the best news of all: within you resides everything you need to be living your best life very soon. This book provides the road map and strategies to take you to the life you were born to live, via the Stage Climbing Solution, in the shortest time possible.

So let's get started. The main premise of Stage Climbing is simple: happiness, inner peace, optimal motivation, and a life determined by your unique passions and purpose and characterized by excellence are all ingredients that define your highest potential. You will soon recognize this zone as a highly accessible part of you, and you will learn how to get there. By eliminating what blocks your path to that zone, you will naturally mature to your highest potential. This is the life you were born to live. Finding and staying on the shortest path to it is the purpose of this book.

Stage Climbing is about you and your life as well as how to take immediate control of it, along with your destiny. It's also about how and why you think and act as you do, how you once were, and how you could be. Stage Climbing will teach you a set of principles to help you understand and deal with anyone who has ever crossed your path or who ever will. You may also find it useful to consider this book as an encyclopedia of choices. In addition to providing you the proverbial "meal," as do most self-help books, it's also my intention that it will teach you "how to fish."

The primary mission of this book is to present you with a concept that is so powerful that it can empower you to understand and then choose to accept or make changes to virtually any area of your life. If you compare yourself to others, Stage Climbing will help you to stop doing that. Instead you will clearly see how to make the only comparison that's truly valid: the one between *your life as it is now* and *what it could be.* You can think of the latter as your highest potential as you now see it. And the sooner you get there, the better your life will be! Merely using the resources that exist within will empower you to reach this goal, or get as close to it as you are willing to go.

One of the great mysteries of the mind is what I call *psychological farsightedness*. Often we cannot see what we're too close to. So I also urge you to consider this book to be a set of psychological reading glasses.

If you are a fan of any of the fine books and programs out there that provide strategies for life change, you'll be happy to know that Stage Climbing is compatible with virtually every one of them. For that reason, don't discard any of your favorite self-help books or audios, even those that may not have yet produced lasting results. Once you learn the Stage Climbing system, you may find a new understanding of how they fit into your life.

Whether you are sitting high atop the pinnacle of success and affluence and trying to make a blessed life even better, in a jail cell where you believe you have little or no control over your life, or anywhere in between, the principles of Stage Climbing are waiting for you to put them into action. Boundless fulfillment, exceptional happiness, and even personal greatness are within everyone's reach. Stage Climbing will give you a system for defining *your* best life, along with the means to get there.

At some point we have all had to rise to the occasion, even if simply to deal with a crisis or to help someone else. Stage Climbing shows you how to make access to those inner resources second nature. In the pages ahead, you'll learn a system that contains seven stages or visions of your-self with respect to just about every important aspect of life.

Emerson said, "We are wiser than we know." Tapping into your own wisdom and ending all forms of self-sabotage is the goal of Stage Climbing. Then watch miracles happen!

Note: For most readers, this book covers all you need to know to incorporate the Stage Climbing system into your life. But mental-health professionals, academicians and researchers, speakers, coaches, and those who simply want more information or a deeper understanding of the Stage Climbing system can find additional resources, strategies, and details about our courses and events at StageClimbing.com.

Stage Climbing brilliantly transforms the best ingredients for reaching your potential into the kind of powerful and highly effective action steps that anyone can apply to quickly make desired life changes.

—STEPHEN R. COVEY,
author of *The 7 Habits of Highly Effective People*

Author's Note

The area of psychology I have always found to be most fascinating is the one that shows how we each develop to become the unique individuals we are and grow to be the best we can be. I help people—often very high achievers— identify their highest potential in one or more parts of their lives, and then do what it takes to make the changes—both within and outside of themselves—to get there as rapidly and effectively as possible.

In the earliest part of my training and career as a psychologist, I first became interested in answering for myself the questions addressed by Stage Climbing. When my daughter was born, like most new parents, I found myself mesmerized by watching her early development. Thus, in graduate school, I studied virtually everything I could find on human development, especially the top theorists and their trademark theories (see "Acknowledgments").

In this process and later on, however, many gaps became evident to me as I was using these ideas when treating clients in the real world. So my mission became twofold: to fill in those gaps and to keep refining my own model, which I now call *Stage Climbing*. I decided I would not be happy until it became as useful a tool for you, the reader, to bring about rapid and lasting change as it has been for me personally and those I have helped with earlier versions. I hope you also will find that it makes the understanding of human behavior, development, maturity, motivation, and how to reach your potential and live your best life easy and enjoyable.

Before writing this book, I also needed to satisfy myself that I could explain just about any aspect of my own life by using the Stage Climbing model. My life has been one of many twists and turns. Stage Climbing meets this challenge and continues to help me understand and navigate the flow of my own life as nothing else ever has. Once you learn the premise and the formula, it will do the same for you.

Most psychologists would probably agree that the practice of psychology is really about teaching people to help themselves, and I have been fortunate enough to see this in action with an extraordinarily wide range of people in many different settings. I have had major contracts to work with both criminals and the police. In my private practice, I have treated patients with severe mental impairments; worked with college students; and helped extremely successful, well-functioning, and highly accomplished clients. In fact, I've had the privilege of working with clients who are some of our highest achievers in business, the professions, education, politics, the media, and even sports. I also have been a consultant to many business, government, and educational organizations and executives, written several popular books, and created many audio programs with major publishers for couples, singles, and those in relationship transitions. My audio self-help programs on numerous personal and relationship topics are used globally by lay people and mental-health professionals alike. I have taught undergraduate and graduate students, trained mental-health professionals extensively, and have even headed an internationally acclaimed training institute. My radio programs have been broadcast locally and nationally. I have appeared on *Oprah* and *The Today Show,* as well as in countless other print and electronic media. Most of all—and I say this with an immeasurable degree of gratitude to all of my patients, clients, readers, trainees, and colleagues—I have enjoyed almost every minute of it!

All the while, I have been working behind the scenes on the concept of Stage Climbing. I decided long ago that I would not write this book until I could definitively say that the theory and practice it espouses holds up with virtually any segment of the population to which it is applied. For over thirty years, I have used evolving versions of Stage Climbing as clinical tools in my practice to help bring about change for thousands of clients who have represented almost every conceivable walk of life. Personally, this included my own roles as a husband (in a very successful second marriage), father, and grandfather, as well as every type of personal or business relationship in which I am involved. And now I bring it to you, with the hope that it will become your personal tool for dramatically and permanently living your best life!

CHAPTER ONE

Life at Your Highest Potential
How Good Can It Be?

The mission of Stage Climbing is to help you live any aspect of your life that you choose to work on at your highest potential. So what is your highest potential? Most simply, it is you at your best and happiest in any given part of your life. This is my definition of Your Best Life! Think about where you could be happier or more fulfilled: relationships, business, career, parenting, spirituality, your life's mission. It's that zone where you're guided by your passions and living beyond your ego—as a grown-up. It's where your body, mind, and spirit are solidly aligned with your purpose. Most importantly, *it's living the life you were born to live.*

Any happy event, success, victory, or windfall can trigger great feelings in you—temporarily. But as you have probably noticed many times, a frame of mind that depends on outside factors that you cannot control does not last. The problem is simply that you are always subject to the next life event, and then the next one, and the one after that. The good news: *As humans, that state of fulfillment is one you can experience at will when you are living life at your highest potential.* And it's actually a natural part of you that, once discovered, will *not fluctuate with external events.* In other words, you have inside of you all you will ever need to be living in that gloriously fulfilling zone right now. Getting there is our mission together.

To the extent that you are committed to living your life—or any part of it—at its highest potential, consider this to be a laundry list that defines your state of mind for that aspect of your life. Some of these things may not resonate with you, but chances are many of them will. So the first step is to decide which of them you would like to make a part of your life and do more of:

- To reach your long-term goals with an exciting openness to new experience, and to connect with others in a more satisfying way.
- To eliminate blame and to forgive your parents, former lovers, bosses, work associates, or anyone else toward whom you still have anger or other negative feelings—including, most importantly, *yourself.*
- To be aware of the infinite number of life choices available to you. To become empowered rather than overwhelmed

by these choices, and never again to allow the expectations of others to override those you have for yourself.

- To trade self-consciousness for a permanent state of self-acceptance that is totally free from what others think of you.

- To make passion your guiding force, along with your purpose and determination.

- To be open on a spiritual level, with purpose, benevolence, and gratitude as your guiding forces.

- To connect directly with God, your higher self, the divine, or whatever you may call upon for your source of higher power—perhaps, but not necessarily, through religion. To know that you have the ability to bypass religion and go directly to that source.

- To become committed to your unique contributions to the world and those around you. To connect to and leave your footprint on things much bigger than yourself.

- To eliminate your fear of the future or death. To be at peace and free of inner conflicts. To be free of self-defeating behavior so that you realize that your own happiness and destiny are in your hands exclusively.

These characteristics all have one thing in common. *They all reside within you at this very moment*, just waiting to be activated and developed. Best of all, you have no competition, so there is nobody you need to overpower or defeat in order to succeed in living your life in this zone.

Within You Are All the Essential Ingredients You Need To Make This Journey in the Shortest Time Possible.

The applications are limitless!

The only way you won't succeed is if you give up!

How do you get there? First, it bears repeating that it's *natural* to have this state of mind. If you're not there now organically, it means you've become stuck along the way. *The Stage Climbing mission is to help you get unstuck.* In some, perhaps most, aspects of life, you may already be unstuck, but in others, you may need to help the process along by clearing away the obstacles that block access to this amazing zone. In addition, by applying the Stage Climbing system, you will empower yourself to master a new tool for making life changes, understanding others around you, managing your emotions, motivating people, and much more!

CHAPTER TWO

The Seven Stages
What They Are and How to Master Them

One can never consent to creep
when one feels an impulse to soar.
—HELEN KELLER

The premise of Stage Climbing is grounded in a well-established principle: *that we humans mature mentally and emotionally in predictable stages,* just as we do physically. In the pages ahead, you will learn about the seven distinct stages of your life. Once you understand how you function at each one, it will become second nature to you to access the best parts of yourself in order to handle almost any situation. Even more importantly, you will know exactly how to enter at will that zone where your highest potential resides, and where you are operating according to your own unique passions and purpose.

As we outgrow or complete one stage, we move on to the next. That's how nature intended it. But for a variety of reasons, we all tend to leave behind parts of ourselves—

The Stage Climbing Premise Is Simple.

It's a well-established fact that *we organically develop in stages.*

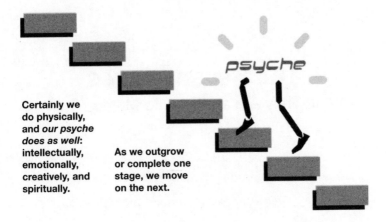

Certainly we do physically, and *our psyche does as well*: intellectually, emotionally, creatively, and spiritually.

As we outgrow or complete one stage, we move on the next.

what I call *hooks*—in each stage. Our hooks to our lower stages are the obstacles that hold us back from organically advancing to the next stage. As you will see, lower-stage hooks can significantly impair your ability to fulfill your dreams, have the quality of relationships you want, and pursue your unique purpose. So identifying, understanding, and managing your lower-stage hooks is the key to reaching your potential and living that passion- and purpose-driven best life you were born to live.

Stages are simply plateaus of development that pinpoint how much you've evolved or matured *in any given life area.* Think of your stages as benchmarks that can explain practically any aspect of who you are or why you do what you do in that part of your life. *Stages are also the most identifiable steps to your best life.* Your seven stages also provide you with fascinating insights about your life—past and present—as well as with strategies for living it optimally in the future.

I will summarize each stage below and will cover them in detail in the chapters ahead. As you read the descriptions of each stage, try to recognize and identify them with various elements of your life and parts of yourself as well as of those around you. Just keep in mind that our complexity as human beings enables you to operate simultaneously at different stages with respect to different parts of your life, such as your career, relationships, parenting, and your social, spiritual, and sexual lives. Most importantly, these seven ascending stages are in reality *the lenses through which you view and experience your life and all of its challenges.*

Now for the stages themselves. Don't worry: my job is to simplify the complex. Your challenge right now is simply to follow each stage, so that by the time we've covered them all you will be able to choose the stage or stages from which you most wish to operate in any given situation or part of your life. And throughout this book, you'll get many strategies and resources to help you get to exactly where you want to be.

Stages One through Four are normal or typical default stages from birth through late adolescence. These first four stages are also the ones that, as an adult, you most likely want to get beyond, wherever you might be stuck. Your

The Stages

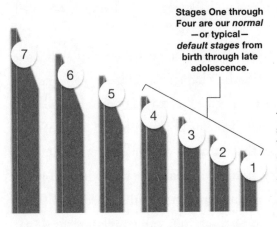

Stages One through Four are our *normal* —or typical— *default stages* from birth through late adolescence.

These first four stages are also the ones that, as an adult, you most likely want to get beyond, wherever you might be stuck.

hooks there—and we all have some—can be problematic, as they often hold us back from experiencing the most fulfilling aspects of our destiny.

Stage One is the only possible stage during infancy. After that, our problematic hooks from Stage One cause us to be overdependent upon others and unable to take initiative— much as we were when we were infants—often resulting in feelings of inadequacy and victimhood.

Stage Two is the normal stage for toddlers, where learning limits is our principal task. Our problematic hooks in Stage Two can thereafter lead us to a life without regard to limits, resulting in primitive and undisciplined behavior and self-centeredness, along with the toddlerlike tendency to act out and create chaos for ourselves and others.

Stage Three is the usual stage through late childhood, where it's important to learn about the rules of living in a civilized society. Thereafter, our problematic Stage Three hooks can leave us to operate as rigid rule abiders or authoritarian personalities, not yet ready to be unique, and extremely inflexible regarding rules and ideas.

Stage Four is the typical stage throughout adolescence. Here we not only form our unique identities but ideally come to accept ourselves for the individuals we've become. As adults, our problematic Stage Four hooks often trigger anxiety, depression, self-doubt, alienation, shame, and self-defeating behavior, as well as excessive approval seeking, perfectionism, fear of failure, and self-consciousness, much like the most difficult aspects of our adolescence.

Stage Five is the normal stage for an adult in our society. At Stage Five, you often think of yourself as a role juggler—the sum of all your life roles, such as what you do in your career and as a spouse, parent, friend, golf partner, or church member. Your characteristic view of life at Stage Five is generally comfortable, dispassionate, or neutral. This stage offers the ideal attitudes and frame of mind to function best while doing what's necessary to keep your life together and functioning. Therefore it's important to have a Stage Five frame of mind with respect to certain relationships and activities as well as to handling many of the tasks necessary for living life in the higher stages. But *normal* is not the same as *ideal*. For example, some people describe particular aspects of this stage as "going through the motions." You can often experience disappointment when you expect higher degrees of fulfillment than this stage can deliver. The result is often overwhelm, stress, and the inability to convert even success or the sense of "having it all" to feelings of happiness or fulfillment.

Stages Six and Seven are the stages where most people aspire to operate. For this reason, I call them your *target stages.* This is you at your best! It's your passion- and purpose-driven best life, where fulfillment and happiness are internally generated. It's the zone of your highest potential. As we saw in the previous chapter, it's the life you were born to live.

As we delve into Stages Six and Seven, you will want to remove anything that blocks your path to the zone where you are naturally and effortlessly operating at your best. Indeed most people view life at these stages as where they feel the very best about themselves, to do what they are here for, and, from a spiritual perspective, to achieve their life's purpose.

Stage Six is in effect the stage of a mature adult. This is determined not by your chronological age, but by the way you conduct your life—with a strong integrity and sense of self. At Stage Six, you rise above your roles and operate according to your own internally generated set of principles, values, and passions. To the extent that these become your driving forces, genuine fulfillment results. This is the stage in which you love, enjoy, excel, create, and connect with spirituality in your own distinct way.

Stage Seven is the highest stage attainable. At Stage Seven, you're beyond *needing* self-gratification. Instead you find fulfillment through your benevolence and your purpose-driven contribution to others and to the world, and from your capacity to act as an agent of change in some large or small way. At Stage Seven, your purpose outside of yourself has more importance to you than what's merely in your own self-interest.

So now you have a taste of the seven stages. In fact, you may have even recognized your default stage, or how you normally operate in the part of your life that's most on your mind. If not, you will soon, as you read more about each stage in the chapters ahead and learn the tools and strategies for navigating, managing, and enjoying the best aspects of each one of them.

You may find that in certain life areas you're already operating at stages Six or Seven—either through your natural and organic Stage Climbing process or the work you've previously done on yourself to get there, while

A Hook . . .

Any part of you that is uncharacteristically in a stage higher or lower than what your "default stage" would indicate.

Some hooks can be beneficial. Others are extremely counterproductive.

Hooks can propel you forward or hold you back.

Think of your hooks as things you sometimes do, feel, or believe that are anomalies or exceptions to how you normally operate.

other areas cry out for change in that direction. Stages Six and Seven are your most *authentic* self. They define you at your best and happiest, because you're guided by your dreams and passions, are living beyond your ego, and are solidly aligned with your purpose. It's where your heart *is*, as opposed to where you or anyone else thinks it should be.

Throughout this book, for the sake of simplicity, I'll at times personify a stage by speaking of *Ones, Twos, Threes, Fours, Fives, Sixes,* and *Sevens* when referring to people characterized by any of these stages. But please keep in mind that it's rare for even a single aspect of someone's life to be totally defined by any one stage, or for anyone to possess all of the traits associated with a given stage. Nevertheless, you may still notice that when you think about certain people, you might tend to brand them by what you perceive as the stage that defines them for you in the area of life where you are most connected to them.

Now let's talk about those parts of yourself that I refer to as your *hooks*. These are the obstacles that you'll invariably encounter on your way to living and enjoying life at the higher stages. Think of your hooks as simply your thoughts, feelings, and/or behaviors that are typical of stages—higher *or* lower—than how you normally operate in a given part of your life. Hooks can always be linked to a specific stage.

To manage your hooks is to identify, understand, neutralize, and/or remove them. If you are not where you want to be, look for the hook that's holding you back. This is an extremely important part of the Stage Climbing process, because it's a key to resolving your most daunting issues as well as finding and living in that zone of your highest potential. The good news is that *taking control of your hooks is a powerful way to take charge of your life.* Understanding and mastering the hooks at each stage not only is quite doable, but will eventually become second nature. Most of the strategies throughout this book will help you systematically do this in an almost paint-by-the-numbers approach.

Sometimes a hook to a lower stage can explain why you have difficulty enjoying life or some important aspect of it. Some hooks are blind spots, meaning that you don't realize you have them, although others around you might. Other hooks you (and sometimes only you) are very much aware of having. In this case, they might be parts of yourself that you *choose* not to change or share with anyone else. As long as it's your choice, you are empowered! I believe that the worthiest goal of all for any part of your life is simply to be both guided by and living by your own *conscious* choices.

Your problematic hooks can keep you stuck at a lower stage. Most commonly, they're what you might call your hang-ups, which tend to cause you problems in your life and hold you back. But also keep this in mind: As you learn more about the stages, you'll find that in some situations, certain lower-stage hooks not only serve you well and work for your benefit, but can even be great resources and sources of strength and enjoyment. So there'll be times when you will choose to access your lower-stage hooks for specific situations. When you do, enjoy them! We'll discuss exactly how this works when covering each stage.

The effect of your hooks can be anywhere from minimal to all-consuming. You can think of some of them as a drop of dark ink in a clear glass of water—coloring your life greatly. Or it can simply be an occasional thought, like a small drop of ink on a large canvas that, if ignored, doesn't have to affect your life at all. Nonetheless, each time you've gained control over any problematic hook, you've not only solved a problem, but broken a pattern as well. And to break a troubling pattern is to change your life! To use a football metaphor: whenever you overcome a troubling or self-defeating pattern, you gain permanent yardage toward that goal of living your best life. The best news of all is that once you learn the Stage Climbing system, this process is totally under your control, and from then on, you can choose to apply it to any part of your life whenever a major change or even a tweak is in order.

We also have hooks to our higher stages. They give us a glimpse of what life can be like as we climb to that zone of our highest potential. These higher-stage hooks help us to propel ourselves upward, like a hook at the end of a rope you're using to pull yourself up a mountain. Just remember what all hooks—lower- or higher-stage, problematic or benign—have in common is simply that they are a part of you in a stage higher or lower than the one in which you normally operate in that part of your life.

Bottom line: relish the hooks that benefit you, and make a commitment to manage, remove, or neutralize the ones that don't. Then watch your natural and organic growth process kick in to deliver you to that zone of your highest potential, guided by your passions and unique purpose.

In the chapters ahead, we'll explore each of the seven stages *as steps to your best life* and their unique challenges and rewards. At each stage, think of a part of yourself with hooks there, now or at some time in the past. Then reflect on how you view an aspect of your life through each of these seven lenses.

You'll probably benefit most by reading the chapters that focus on the seven stages in order—at least the first time you read them. The downside and upside of each stage is presented in detail. *At times, certain aspects of the first four stages may be especially painful or difficult to read about as they pertain to you or someone close to you.* But stay with it, and it'll all come together by the time you've read about all seven.

Whether this book will become a life-changing event for you or will merely be a good read is up to you. Learning powerful theory and state-of-the-art techniques is not quite enough. The action steps, and your commitment to take the ones that speak to you, are the ingredients this process needs to maximally work its magic for you.

So here's a powerful assumption to take with you to the chapters ahead: with the right information, strategies, and will, there's very little you can't overcome or achieve. This book will provide the information and strategies; all you need to bring is the will and, of course, the relentless commitment to make your life *exactly* what you want it to be!

CHAPTER THREE

Stage One
Overcoming Dependency

There's a somebody I'm longing to see, I hope that he
turns out to be, someone to watch over me
—GEORGE AND IRA GERSHWIN,
"SOMEONE TO WATCH OVER ME"

Before getting to the exciting stuff that's waiting for you in Stages Six and Seven—for a vision of your best life—it's important to learn about the lower stages. Through these next few chapters, you'll soon recognize the things that, up until now, have been blocking your access to this zone as an effortless part of your growth process. Although much of what you'll hear about may not apply to you *right now*, it could help you to better understand certain people around you; it could also explain aspects of who you were in an earlier era of your life. For this reason, you'll notice that I often talk in the third person about those in the lower stages.

Moreover, the things that you do recognize about yourself may be a bit difficult or even painful to read about at times. But it's important to go there in order to recognize and gain control of present self-sabotaging and problematic hooks. Then your natural Stage Climbing process can kick in and take you to that zone where you're living by your purpose and passions.

So let's go right to Stage One.

The Stage One challenge is to *overcome dependency, powerlessness,* and *victimhood* that hold you back. In this chapter, we'll explore these issues and how to remove them as obstacles to living your best life.

Picture yourself on a paradise island, with people waiting on you hand and foot. You are being thoroughly pampered and don't have a care or need in the world that isn't being satisfied by someone else. Nice image? People pay a lot of money for that feeling on a vacation. Kings have conquered countries to provide aspects of this lifestyle for themselves, their families, and a privileged few. Having all of your needs attended to by others can also be thought of as the definition of *ideal infant care.*

This is an example of Stage One at its best. Even though it's a great fantasy, and sometimes we may long for it when life gets overwhelming or stressful, few adults can or would consciously choose to remain in that state indefinitely.

Stage One begins at birth and is the normal, in fact the only, stage of development we are capable of during infancy—for the first year or two of life. So in the Stage One world, the infant and those who play the role of caretaker and wish granter are truly all there is. Early on, infants perceive anyone who enters their world as extensions of themselves, who exist merely to satisfy their needs. For infants, who totally depend on others for just about everything, Stage One *is* their highest potential.

Recently I observed two excellent illustrations of typical Stage One behavior while walking through the park. The first was an infant sitting on its mother's lap on a park bench, cooing and smiling at passersby, who responded warmly. Just a few feet away, a disheveled street person—who, incidentally, appeared to be completely unaware of the baby—sat on another bench, making gestures virtually identical to the baby's. Those passersby who had any response at all to this man reacted with disgust. These same people reacted to the same behavior in profoundly opposite ways because of one thing only—the appropriateness of the ages of the man and the baby with respect to what each was doing. This extreme, yet observable, example illustrates an important aspect of Stage Climbing: what works at one age can be quite inappropriate, even odd, at another. Examples of this can be found at every stage.

Sometimes we also revert to Stage One in old age toward the end of life, when we are needy, sick, or infirm. Your hooks to this stage help you to adjust to having others take care of you—whether you choose to or not. In other

Stage One begins at birth and is our normal, in fact the only, stage of development we are capable of during *infancy*—the first year or two of life.

Illustrations of typical Stage One behavior.

Sometimes we also revert to Stage One in old age toward the end of life, when needy, sick, or infirm.

phases of life, your Stage One hooks enable you to receive without needing to give back in kind. They can even trigger joyous feelings when letting yourself be pampered by your significant other, at a spa, or while on vacation.

The stages illustrate how the maturation process plays out naturally and organically. They will also reveal some of the major factors that influence how you mature mentally and emotionally as you age chronologically. For infants and others operating at Stage One, parents and caretakers are obviously the critical others. Ideally, the best age-appropriate care consists of unconditional love and nurturing during the first years of life, without expecting much in return.

If, however, adults become stuck emotionally in Stage One beyond infancy, they will continue to operate as though they, along with those who enable them, were the whole world. Extreme dependency, even helplessness, can become a way of life. This is the dark side of Stage One. Sadly, the result could be a wasted life. This exaggerated dependency could also underlie the symptoms of some of the most severe forms of mental disorders.

Stuck in this stage, Ones can become chronically needy and dependent, severely narcissistic and self-centered, or addicted to harmful substances, or they may have many or all of these characteristics together.

As we explore each of the seven stages, you will read many quotations from my notes from sessions with actual people I've worked with. *All names and other identifying information have been changed, and the quotes have been paraphrased for the purpose of confidentiality and clarity.* Here is a sampling of how some people I've worked with have seen themselves through the lens of Stage One:

Judith: "I had no incentive to leave my parents' home and make a life of my own until I met a spouse who enabled my behavior as much as my parents did. Needless to say, the marriage didn't last very long. I abhorred the dependent side of me so much that I even began to resent anyone who tried to help me."

Barbara: "I was in a highly abusive marriage with a man I certainly admit I'd have never married in the first place if he hadn't been a good provider. We had a lot of money and great social status. I was actually envied by others and seen as having a blessed life, free of conflict and hassle. I thought I would have an easy life, yet it was anything but. I began to hate my life and even worse, to hate myself for being unable or, as I see it now, *unwilling* to take the risk and leave. When I finally left, none of my friends or family could understand how I could leave that 'blessed' lifestyle until I explained that the only thing keeping me there were my chronic feelings of inadequacy!"

Some men marry women whom they perceive as extensions of their mothers: someone to cook for them, clean up after them, and take care of all of life's annoyances, leaving them free to pursue their careers and hobbies. And of course there are those who marry someone wealthy for merely materialistic reasons. These types of relationships—and many variations of them—are far from uncommon. When they're grounded more in fear-based Stage One hooks than simply desire or conscious choice, they often end as it becomes apparent that there is a lack of the passion, intimacy, and friendship that characterize the best long-term relationships.

On the other hand, there are times or circumstances when hooks in Stage One can enhance your life. They serve you, for example, when it's your choice to be lazy, carefree, or childlike. A nice win-win aspect of the best friendships and love relationships is the delightful experience of sometimes being taken care of without the need to give back on a quid pro quo basis. Stage One play for adults is self-pampering: letting yourself be totally taken care of on a vacation at an all-inclusive resort or a luxury cruise, being pampered at a spa, or even enjoying downtime by lying on a hammock in your backyard with a cold beer on a hot day. These represent healthy and desirable uses for Stage One hooks that you probably would never choose to change.

In addition, sometimes we go back to our lower stages during periods of extreme stress or illness, or at other times even by choice. Our hooks also help us interact with and understand others who are operating out of that stage. When we use our hooks or the insights learned through them for these purposes, they serve us well; but when we believe that we are *unable to choose* to function at the higher stages, our hooks become hang-ups that impair our relationships, life goals, and attitudes. Finally, some people, regardless of how evolved they might have been previously, revert to Stage One late in life as part of age-related mental or physical decline, or even by choice in retirement. And the vision of living a very easy and carefree Stage One–like existence in later years is often a great motivator for saving money long before retirement.

Bottom line: Make *sure that your hooks are there to serve you, never to rule you!*

If we think of a computer as a metaphor for the mind, beliefs constitute the operating system. Our beliefs create anger in us when someone treats us poorly, make us feel anxious when faced with a difficult challenge, or cause depression when we fail at something important. In the Stage Climbing process, we replace beliefs that underlie problematic hooks with beliefs consistent with the life we are striving for. The more you do this, the more your operating system will reflect the choices you have made as an adult rather than the self-defeating assumptions that may have been with you since long before you can remember.

Happiness and success at Stage One can be defined as a life that's easy and effortless, with no demands or challenges, along with a reliable and dependable provider of all necessities. But as the adage goes, "There's no free lunch." An adult lifestyle that is grounded in dependency on others can obviously have very high costs in one's quality of life.

You may be stuck in Stage One if some of these attitudes and beliefs govern you in one or more parts of your life:

- "I am inadequate."
- "I am helpless."
- "I can't do it."
- "Life is too hard, so I must be taken care of."
- "I must have someone else to satisfy me and care for my every need."
- "I am a victim."
- "It's no use for me even trying to make things better."

- "I must be certain that any decision I make is the right one or I won't able to handle the consequences."
- "I cannot take charge of my own life."
- "If I took initiative and failed, I wouldn't be able to handle it."
- "I have no choices that will make my life better."
- "I am unable to overcome my past or upbringing. What's happened to me in the past (e.g., my childhood) makes it impossible for me to take charge of my life."

John, a retail-store manager: "I was laid off from my job and got a little too comfortable on unemployment. For a while, I actually lost my ambition and incentive to succeed. What I surprisingly discovered when my unemployment ran out was that with the incentive to *underachieve* gone, my motivation returned. Had I been able to rely on unemployment indefinitely, I might have gotten comfortable enough to give up on ambition altogether or put it on the back burner—permanently."

John was then able to get back on his path by finding a job that would be a stepping-stone to what he really wanted to do. He made a five-year plan and, most importantly, learned valuable lessons about the real cost of dependency, taking charge of his life, and living it in the higher stages. Dependency often starts out of necessity and then morphs into a way of life. Many have told me that they felt the same thing that John experienced when they relied on alimony, welfare, or other types of conditional entitlements. When these are gone, you have a choice between assuming the posture of victimhood and making your life over in a way that's self-sufficient.

Like infants, Ones often lack the concept of being able to get up and do something to help themselves.

- Joan: "I was actually at my best emotionally when I was sick and my roommates cheerfully took care of me. Once I was able to see this as a Stage One hook, I actually stopped getting sick so often!"

- Bill: "My drinking and drug abuse were obviously self-medication, which acted as anesthesia for the inevitable pain of feeling powerless. For several years, it was only when I was high that I could get glimpses of how life could be. That's what kept my addiction going."

- Sue: "I could never handle conflict. I just walked away whenever anything upset me and went right to self-pity, until I had no more marriage and almost no friends and couldn't keep a job. I finally realized that the problem wasn't everyone else, it was me. That realization was the first step in turning my life around by refusing to be a victim any longer."

For Sue, giving up victimhood was a major step. When you think of yourself as a victim—of a bad marriage, childhood traumas, social injustice, or almost anything else—the pain of your wounds can overpower everything. *Instead, work toward turning those wounds into scars.* Scars are wounds that have healed and are therefore no longer a source of pain. The object is not to forget your wounds, but to make them benign so that they no longer consume your energy or hold you back.

One of the most common Stage One hooks is the inability to make important decisions or sometimes even to make decisions at all. *Indecisiveness is little more than a demand for certainty,* and certainty in any form is a myth. After all, would any decision would be difficult if you were certain of the outcome? So this hook can keep you stuck and feeling helpless, which then becomes a nasty vicious circle, where you tell yourself that there's no use even trying!

Psychologists have long recognized that there is little, if any, correlation between maturity and intelligence. Thus it's not at all unusual to be stuck at Stage One or at any stage in a given area of life while still being exceptionally bright and functioning remarkably well in other parts of your life. Once you turn those problematic hooks into choices, you take full control of your life.

Many folktales reflect this process: the protagonists move from some form of "slavery" to freedom, and experience the joy of taking charge of their own destiny— bringing about the archetypal happy ending. And life rarely gets better than that!

Climbing out of Stage One: What You Need to Know

First and foremost, it bears repeating, and please remind yourself of this often: *blaming your parents, spouse, boss, opponents, detractors, or anyone else for what you perceive as your predicament will only keep you stuck there!*

The first step in passing through any of the lower stages is to acknowledge and take responsibility for your hooks there, but *without berating yourself any further* for having them. In return for refusing to blame yourself or others, here is the good news: *any initiative that you decide to take on your own is a step toward permanent change.*

Becoming proactive and self-sufficient in any area of your life in which you may have defined yourself as being powerless or stuck is the core of beginning the Stage Climbing process out of Stage One. You just have to commit to it and remember to do it.

In Stage One, the greatest challenge is taking the initiative. Judith, whom we met earlier in the chapter, describes the belief that kept her stuck in dependency: "I constantly told myself, *'Nothing I do will make things better for me, so why even try?'* It was astounding to discover that believing things like this was what held me back and made me feel so inadequate. Everything and everyone else I blamed impacted me the way it did because of that attitude." Indeed Judith's toxic belief (along with the others discussed earlier) become the self-fulfilling prophecies that, left unchallenged, can keep any part of your life stuck at Stage One indefinitely.

For Judith, challenging this dysfunctional belief by setting some attainable goals and choosing new attitudes like "My life is in my hands now" and "It's possible, and up to me and me alone, to live a happy and fulfilling life" gave her the fuel for leaving her dysfunctional marriage, going back to school, and pursuing her dream of being a graphic designer. It also went a long way towards converting her wounds to painless scars. She can still learn from them, but they no longer have to be a source of suffering.

Here are some more of the attitudes that are most helpful for climbing out of Stage One:

- "I can now do what I need to do, though it might sometimes be challenging."
- "I am tired of being dependent and relying on others. I now want to begin taking charge of my own life."
- "I am no longer a victim. I choose to be free of my past, wherever it limits me."
- "The only thing that's certain is that certainty does not exist."
- "I can handle the consequences and outcomes for my decisions, even when they don't turn out the way I hoped they would."
- "Sometimes what is necessary isn't the easiest, safest, or most comfortable choice."

- "Life can be difficult, but it's manageable. It's merely difficult right now, and that's a challenge I can and will handle."

Here are some strategies and action steps for climbing and navigating through Stage One. For the sake of clarity, both here and in subsequent chapters the strategies are numbered.

1. Pick the statements from the list above that speak to you the most, and feel free to add to this list or create your own. Customize them to fit your situation exactly. Write them on a three-by-five-inch card, input them into your smartphone, or place them wherever you can most easily access them. Consider them the affirmations to get you past Stage One and onto the path to your highest potential. The surest way to imprint these beliefs in your mind so that they become second nature is actually *to live by them*. At first this may seem difficult, but if you act as if they were a natural part of you, soon they will be!

Note: The appendix at the end of this book will guide you through this particular exercise in much greater detail, as it does with all of the stages. In addition, we will revisit it as it applies to each of the stages that contain problematic hooks in the next four chapters.

2. Focus on taking some steps in the right direction. Make a list under the heading: "If I were taking the initiative to

take charge of my life, I'd _____," and write down the specific steps you need to begin moving toward your goal. Make your list as comprehensive as possible. Then begin to put this plan into action. For example, get information about going to school; seek an independent financial opinion to help you evaluate the feasibility of leaving your marriage; update your résumé; start looking for an apartment; do the networking you've been putting off.

For many, dependency can be extremely hard to give up—especially if someone important in your life enables you to stay in your current situation or serves as an ongoing obstacle to change, such as in a controlling or abusive relationship. For example, many parents unwittingly enable their adult children to stay in the Stage One zone by encouraging them to live at home for far too long. Therefore more than half the battle is to realize how important it is to commit to and follow through with any step you take out of your comfort zone. The freedom to discover worlds you would otherwise never know exist is waiting for your discovery. It lies on the other side of the wall that keeps you stuck at Stage One.

Barbara, whom we also met earlier in this chapter as she described her abusive marriage, said this of her climb out of Stage One: "When I realized that happiness and all the hopes and dreams associated with it were unattainable because of a Stage One hook, I knew I had to climb out of my 'crib' and make things happen or I would be trapped there forever. So before doing anything drastic, I consulted a divorce attorney and a financial adviser. They were able to address my legal and financial fears. I then made a detailed to-do list. When the time was right and I had a place to move to, I informed my husband (my lawyer suggested that I not be alone when I do this, because of his temper) and moved to my new place. I feel as if I'd gotten my life back and it was now my own! If I could do it in the frame of mind I started with, anyone can. Now I believe that anything I become committed to—difficult as it may be—is possible."

Most importantly, listen to those moments of awakening when you realize that whether or not you achieve a desire or reach a goal *is up to you and no one else!*

3. Visualize your life without the safety net that may be holding you back from taking the reins. Then do something—anything—that brings you even one small step toward breaking free of a toxic comfort zone, or what I call a comfortable stage of discomfort. For example: actually start looking for the job you really want; ask someone out for a date; say good-bye to someone toxic in your life; get an up-to-date graduate-school catalog or go online and explore the program you dream of pursuing; set some solid goals and line up a support group to help you tackle them. In addition to all of the other benefits, each time you accomplish something you set out to do, you prove to yourself that you can!

I have seen many people in my practice like Barbara, for whom necessity or some form of adversity forced them to climb out of Stage One. For example, the death of, or divorce from, someone on whom they heavily depended may have required them to take on tasks, missions, and goals they might have otherwise avoided. If this hits home, you may be shocked at what you can accomplish if only you become committed to trying. For me, this is always an inspiring phenomenon to watch.

But you don't have to wait for crisis or necessity to make this choice. The climb out of Stage One is an option available to you anytime, and it applies to any aspect of your life.

Numerous additional strategies for managing your Stage One hooks can be found at StageClimbing.com.

CHAPTER FOUR

Stage Two
Taming Your Primitive Self

I did not have sexual relations with that woman.
—BILL CLINTON

This quote may be remembered more than anything else Bill Clinton said during his eight-year presidency. It illustrates how strongly Stage Two behavior by public figures can resonate.

The main Stage Two challenge is to learn how to take charge of your impulses and inhibitions. Sometimes that means setting limits as well as becoming more disciplined. At other times, however, you may need to *lower* your inhibitions so that you can experience joy!

Imagine that you are the center of the universe, much as you did with Stage One. Only this time you have the ability and energy to get up off your chair and take anything you want. Imagine that no one else has any feelings or needs, as if they were expendable toys. There are no rules to follow, so there are no consequences for taking or destroying anything that stands in your way. Have a tantrum, and the world satisfies you by delivering whatever it is you are screaming for. Then everything is just fine until you want something else, and when you do, no problem—just find a way to demand or take that too. It's all yours for the asking, or taking.

That's essentially the mind-set of the toddler, and if our species required no other rules or standards for discipline, that would be humankind in a nutshell.

Perhaps in primitive times, when we had more in common psychologically with other species of mammals, it was. Life was good until some stronger or smarter "toddler" preyed upon you. Thus a good one-word description of the anarchy of Stage Two is *primitive*. We were all there once—personally as toddlers and maybe in prehistoric times as a species—and, most of us on occasion still revisit this part of our lives by virtue of our Stage Two hooks.

Now imagine a toddler with the physical and intellectual capabilities of an adult, and you have an unvarnished profile of a genuine Two. What a life! For a humorous rendition of adults celebrating Stage Two anarchy, watch any Marx Brothers or Three Stooges film. It's the spectacle of adults behaving like toddlers that makes these characters so hilarious. For a look at adult Twos that are not so funny, go to any

Stage Two

Stage Two is the normal and typical stage for toddlers, where learning limits is our principal task. Our *problematic hooks* in Stage Two can thereafter lead us to a life without regard to limits.

+ Primitive and highly undisciplined behavior
+ Self-centeredness
+ Tendency to act out and create much chaos for ourselves and others

movie or TV show that features a one-dimensional criminal or sociopath preying on someone to get what they want without regard for anyone but themselves.

Stage Two normally begins somewhere between the ages of one and two and lasts about two years. This is the stage of development where, as toddlers, motivated by a combination of curiosity and a newfound ability to be mobile, we first begin to discover our environment and to shift our focus toward what's going on outside of ourselves.

At Stage Two, we are naturally uninhibited, playful, and joyous, and these traits become the Stage Two hooks we will probably want to preserve throughout our lives. Toddlers can now become aware of and interact with other people in addition to caretakers. Since, for the first time, they are mobile, they also have the ability and a natural tendency—as the parent of any toddler can tell you—to begin to test the limits.

Children at this stage need to become aware that other people have feelings too, and to learn that others are not extensions of themselves, nor are they merely there to serve them. This is the time to learn how to have fun, but also to accept the reality of the biggest inconvenient fact of all: that *nobody gets everything they want all of the time.* Stage Twos don't yet buy into this unpleasant reality.

We gradually and organically pass through Stage Two throughout the fourth year of life. However, there are two possible consequences of insufficiently passing through this stage: One is the danger of developing a sense of shame and self-doubt, which is to say that the child could become afraid to exercise almost any kind of initiative at all. This is in reality an emotional detour back to Stage One.

More commonly, being stuck at Stage Two can result in a varying degree of disregard for rules and limits altogether. For toddlers, play normally involves learning about the world *their* way, and that means whatever is fun suits them. Since toddlers love to explore, they are not yet concerned with the consequences of their behavior. They are easily bored and tend to do or take whatever appeals to them in whatever way they can. In other words, anything they can get away with is a victory. With this in mind, it's easy to see how strong hooks at this stage can result in extreme and perhaps dangerous risk taking and rebellious and even criminal behavior as an adult—once again, without any regard to consequences.

Stage Two Hooks You Hopefully Want to Keep

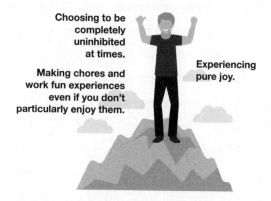

Choosing to be completely uninhibited at times.

Making chores and work fun experiences even if you don't particularly enjoy them.

Experiencing pure joy.

One of the most reliable ingredients for leading the best possible life is to make the most of your hooks from each stage, the parts that add good things to your life. It's quite healthy, desirable, and a lot of fun at any age to hedonistically play hard and, under the right circumstances, to be completely uninhibited. This is a great example of how we can call upon our Stage Two hooks to serve us as adults. For example, many couples describe their best and most uninhibited sex as wildly enjoyable and ecstatic. Certainly this is the result of a healthy and desirable Stage Two hook. Thus, in the higher stages, when you are having fun, experiencing pure joy and even making your work a fun experience, you are choosing to be motivated in those moments in part by your Stage Two hooks. Over the years, I've helped many people to access and become comfortable with that part of themselves in order to let go of unwanted and unnecessary inhibitions.

Howard and Tracey are one of those couples. They say, "Our sex life had become extremely dull. What turned things around was an experiment where we decided to spend an hour pretending we had no inhibitions at all. This resulted in our having the best sex we had in years. Now we build on this and do it regularly. And sex is becoming more and more blissful."

On the other hand, adults with strong Stage Two hooks may also become extremely self-centered and narcissistic, or even sociopathic. People of this kind have some similarities to those at Stage One. The difference is that Stage Two narcissism does not come with helplessness and inaction. Instead, Stage Twos can believe they're entitled to money, power, and sex, and that they can and must have or be able to do anything they want.

Joe, a client of mine who had recently gotten out of prison for dealing drugs, said, "I never had any real role models. Then I finally realized that I was still a young child in many ways or was at least emulating one, who believed I was entitled to act out in whatever way suited me, regardless of the effect my actions had on other people or what others thought about me. I now know that this was a recipe for disaster. I'd lie, steal, bully, distort, or even be violent to get what I wanted, because I believed I *deserved* whatever I craved."

Like their toddler "role models," adult Twos will often do what their immediate and short-term desires crave, sim-

ply because they can. And often Stage Two hooks are profoundly self-defeating.

Cheryl: "I lost almost everything I had gambling. I re-
fused to think of it as an addiction, but certainly couldn't
control it. Excessive gambling wreaked havoc on every part
of my life. I lost everything except for the adrenalin rush
that the action triggered in the moment. Yet in every other
part of my life, I was very much in control. With the help
of Gamblers Anonymous and some good friends I met
there, I finally realized that I absolutely couldn't gamble
at all, ever again, under any circumstances or in any form.
In other words, my choice was clear: to abstain or let gambling completely ruin my life and my future. So far I've
managed to avoid the temptations, and I'm happy to say
they are getting fewer and weaker."

The same can be said for drug and alcohol abuse, as well
as other types of addiction that ignore the long-term cost of
short-term gratification. Twos who use harmful substances
usually do it for recreational purposes (as opposed to Ones,
who use them merely to self-medicate or give themselves
some relief from painful aspects of life). Whenever you do
things you later regret as part of an addiction, look for the
problematic Stage Two hook that pushes you to satisfy your
short-term needs at the cost of what is *ultimately* in your
best interest.

Bob: "I constantly had to relieve my boredom. And yes,
I was bored with life and couldn't stand it. Cocaine pro-

vided the answer I was looking for. When I was high, I was happy, fun, and sociable, and life was easy. But then drugs, along with my drinking, took on a life of its own. I wised up just in time, after getting some bad medical news. I'm now clean and feel lucky to be alive."

Stage Two hooks can indeed take you to some very dark places. Because Stage Twos have little or no regard for the feelings or rights of others, they can commonly engage in criminal behavior. Embezzlers, con artists, other types of thieves and predators, as well as premeditated murderers (if there is also a tendency toward violence), have the most extreme and out-of-control hooks in Stage Two. The ultimate Two could be a serial killer who could take a human life merely in order to get a minute of sexual pleasure for himself. This is arguably humankind at its worst. If our most popular movies and TV shows or the crime novels we read are any indication, our society has been endlessly fascinated by Stage Two characters and their ability to harm unsuspecting victims.

Sal: "What drove me was survival. Also, I hated to work and took advantage of every opportunity to lure people in and then swindle them with phony investment deals. Until I was caught and had to do time, it never even occurred to me that there was anything wrong, since I rationalized that anyone who was dumb enough to let themselves be scammed in this way would be scammed by someone, so it might as well be me. I realized I don't ever want to go back to jail. But until I did, nobody could tell me anything."

Having worked with criminals early in my career, I can tell you that many Twos can be described as the "ultimate free souls." They are free of the need for self-discipline. Instant gratification and avoiding any pain in the moment are all there is. Often Twos can skillfully be whatever they have to be at a given moment to get the result they want. This is one reason that Twos function better than in prison than those at any other stage. They actually feel most at home in an institution that, at its best, is designed to instill limits and provide remedial discipline. It is an adult version of what offenders may not have been able to take in as young children.

Most of us have a killer instinct that we use very rarely. Perhaps we reserve it for such times as when a mosquito is buzzing around our ears on a hot summer night while we are trying to sleep. However, some Twos do not differentiate between an annoying mosquito and a *human* adversary. Vivid examples include the behavior of longtime Stage Two "icons" such as Charles Manson, Ted Bundy, Al Capone, John Dillinger, Bonnie Parker, and Clyde Barrow. They and their mesmerizing fictional counterparts (e.g., Tony Soprano and Vito Corleone) are only a few notable examples of the way Twos can interact with the world when they are on top of their game.

Nevertheless, Twos can blend in easily and can appear to be much like the rest of us. This is no doubt due to their ability to charm us and mimic emotions (rather than experiencing true ones) until their dark sides become apparent, as we have seen from the examples of extreme Stage Two behavior above. But practically all of us have some Stage Two hooks that we may want to take a look at. Just as having hooks in Stage One doesn't make you helpless, having Stage Two hooks doesn't make you bad.

In fact, most of us have some hooks in all of the stages. So it's normal to occasionally display at least minor variations of Stage Two. You may occasionally cheat at cards or throw a tantrum when you don't get your way. Perhaps you sometimes lie or exaggerate to achieve an end or to protect yourself from some unwanted consequence. You may purposely run a red light or evade a tollbooth. Or you may take some undeserved credit, be unfaithful to your spouse, or run your business in a dubious manner. These are choices you may or may not regret.

I'm a psychologist, not a moral philosopher. Thus it's my job to help you to live the life you choose and to help you take complete charge of it. Indeed I've spent practically my entire career helping people find the liberation that comes from replacing self-sabotaging beliefs, attitudes, and behavior with conscious choices. So with Stage Two hooks, my focus is to encourage you to look at your behavior and its long-term consequences. Then you are empowered to decide what's in your best interest to continue or change.

Only you can determine, in your heart of hearts and in the privacy of your own mind, what you're comfortable with and what your limits are when it comes to acting on your Stage Two hooks (or anything else, for that matter). But in reality, it's only when you realize what's to *your* advantage to change that true change occurs.

Sal, the former investment scam artist: "I made a living by selling phony securities, often to older people who could be hurt the most by what I did. Until I woke up spiritually and realized that there could be consequences beyond the obvious ones in this life, I was only capable of survival. That helped me to clean up my life and get onto a decent path, which I now know has far more rewards than I could have imagined back then!"

Joe, a former drug dealer who had also served a prison term: "My answer to any conflict, in a relationship or anywhere else, was to fight and overpower—and I could be very nasty, even abusive—or leave. It never occurred to me that there was any other way to handle things." Joe is typical in that a Stage Two reaction to conflict is generally one of fight or flight, or a combination of them—that is, to lash out or run away if at all possible. Thinking that the other person could have a valid point of view (particularly if it conflicts with their own) is not considered as an option when operating from this stage.

At Stage Two, conflict is typically handled by using some form of deception, a strong-arm tactic, or doing whatever you have to do, without limits, to ensure that you get your way. When acting on Stage Two hooks, you might be extremely charming to manipulate someone, quite brutal to bully or force them, or a combination of these: you will use whatever it takes to get what you want. Twos can also use their intelligence and ability to charm, mimic sincerity, and "learn the system." But in reality, fulfilling their own needs is their only true purpose in life. Happiness at Stage Two is simply a matter of getting your way, regardless of the effect your actions have on anyone or anything else. Success at this stage can usually be defined as getting away with something—whether it's a scam or merely putting something over on someone.

Joe: "Until I decided to turn my life around after being incarcerated and giving up drugs, the world was my oyster. I was very good at manipulating, deceiving, controlling, and overpowering people in almost any situation."

The beginning of conscience, where long-term consequences, along with the realization that others have needs as well, signals the end of Stage Two for toddlers as well as adults with problematic Stage Two hooks. You can change the patterns that result from your Stage Two hooks at any time. It just takes your recognition and the commitment to do so.

To manage your problematic Stage Two hooks, first, recognize which of these attitudes and beliefs about yourself may govern you in one or more parts of your life:

- "I must always enjoy myself and have and do whatever I want, regardless of the effect on others. Life should be easy for me."

- "I don't want to change. The other person (people, or the world) should change."

- "I cannot stand frustration or discomfort. I do things simply because I can and don't concern myself with long-term consequences. I won't change or alter my behavior even if I know it's the right thing to do."

- "People in my life are merely resources for money, sex, power, cover, or position. They are to be exploited or preyed upon."

- "The best way to handle your conscience (if you have one) is to ignore it."

- "I will be or do or say whatever I have to in order to get what I want at any given moment or in any given situation."

- "I must always be treated well; anyone who doesn't is just asking for revenge."

These are some of the most common underlying attitudes and beliefs behind your problematic Stage Two hooks. Take a moment to identify and customize your own variations of these themes. If any of them speak to you, take note and decide which of them you're committed to changing. Try to identify what you are telling yourself or believing when you act on one of your self-defeating Stage

Two hooks. Most importantly, how have they affected your relationships, your career, or other essential areas of your life? Only you know the answer to this question, so you owe it to yourself to ponder it.

One of my clients, Nathan, is a prime example. I've treated many offenders just like him. He confided that "lying, cheating, acting in any way that suited me and conning people increasingly become second nature for me. In fact, deception was my most comfortable way of life; hard work was something to be avoided at all costs. I could never learn from my own mistakes. The criminal justice system was my wake-up call. In jail, I met many people that for one reason or another were beyond help. Fortunately, I made the decision to change before it was too late."

Nathan initially considered the punishment and other adverse consequences he encountered to be the problem, rather than his own criminal behavior. Fortunately for him, prison was the wake-up call he needed, and he was able to turn his life around. This is not always the case. Twos may be able to succeed temporarily by virtue of their charm or intelligence. Even here, however, most Twos will eventually fail unless they get that wake-up call and take massive action as Nathan did. Thus, in addition to being a dark stage, Stage Two can also be quite a self-destructive one.

Less extreme (but often as troubling) Stage Two behavior is also a part of many workplaces. Look for the Stage Two hooks in those who grab credit for successes they have little or nothing to do with, while dodging the blame for other things for which they may have been completely responsible. It is common to encounter people who have little regard for the impact of their behavior on colleagues, no matter how loyal or undeserving of trouble they may be.

Take Marge, for example: "I left a job I otherwise loved because my boss was an unsavory executive who sexually harassed certain female subordinates and constantly bullied his male subordinates. He was so toxic and so feared that he even managed to intimidate people out of filing well-deserved complaints against him."

Then there are the Bernard Madoffs of the world, whose illegal financial schemes and other white-collar predations can affect anyone in their orbit. A case such as Madoff's is high-profile only because of the astoundingly large amount of money he swindled. These types of Stage Two practices are far from uncommon.

Showman P.T. Barnum famously said, "There's a sucker born every minute." By all accounts, he himself operated at much higher stages. Yet Barnum's philosophy of why the masses will come to seek entertainment based on illusion remains part of the "mission statement" of many Twos who are businesspeople, politicians, and others whose success appears to depend on exploiting others.

Stage Two politicians, for example, are out for whatever their can grab or steal, with little or no consideration for their constituencies or the needs of anyone else. Like most Twos, they know just how to exploit individuals, groups, or crowds that can be the source of their money, power, and acclaim. They do this by imitating the desired emotions or the necessary image and by projecting such traits as warmth without having so much as a warm bone in their body. But like Twos in any occupation, they can also be highly abusive in private when the cameras are turned off.

Kathy: "My pattern was to pick men who swept me off my feet with a great first impression. Typically, they seemed to be lot of fun and looked like everything I was looking for, until I got to know them. Most actually turned out to be empty suits, out to get whatever they could and offering little in return. At one point, I sincerely doubted that there were any good men left! Then I wised up and gave a new man I met the chance to grow on me, as opposed to rejecting him because he didn't make a killer first impression. As silly as this may sound now, my negative view of men— treating me as merely a source of sex, sometimes money, an object from whom to suck energy—has completely turned around. I'm now in a long-term relationship, but I definitely had to grow up first myself before being able to get involved with a grown-up."

Philip: "I was sexually promiscuous in my marriage and cheated on my wife left and right. It was fine for *me* to be that way, but I would have never tolerated any infidelity from my wife. For years, I could lie my way out of any-thing, act contrite or charming, and even blame her for not trusting me whenever I needed to get myself out of a crisis. Finally she had enough and left me. I then accepted the fact that I had a problem and got treatment for my sexual addiction. It's too late now to save my marriage, but I now realize the negative consequences I caused, not only to my marriage, but to myself personally."

In my practice, I have heard many variations of both Kathy's and Philip's Stage Two relationship experiences. As Philip explained, when someone they still want in their lives has had enough and is threatening to leave, Twos can often act or mimic being very contrite and concilia-tory until that person is back in their camp. But as soon as the crisis is over, they can be expected to return to their old ways until the next predictable crisis occurs. In Philip's case, this happened many times until his wife made it clear that reconciliation was no longer possible. His case is quite typical: it took the burning of a bridge to something he valued to trigger a sufficient degree of pain to motivate him to change.

Climbing out of Stage Two: What You Need to Know

It's unusual for people who exhibit extreme Stage Two be-havior to seek help on their own accord, or for that matter even to be reading a book like this. But at this point you are likely to be thinking about some of your Stage Two hooks or the Twos you have had to deal with in your life (and may be wondering how to avoid them in the future).

You may have a history of failed relationships, losing jobs, or losing money that you can't afford to lose, for example by excessive gambling. With your commitment to break this pattern, you can quickly turn it around. Therefore, to dismantle problematic Stage Two hooks, begin by identifying those hooks and taking responsibility for them, and then making a vow to choose a different way to live your life. With that in mind, here are some Stage Two action steps:

1. Sometimes part of the process is actually to experience guilt or shame in order to help connect with or strengthen your conscience. Keep in mind that this is the *only* stage where emotions such as guilt and shame can actually be good sources of insight. Usually at the other stages, those feelings are clearly seen as self-destructive, so we strive to weaken or overcome them.

2. It's crucial to first recognize exactly what's in it *for you* to change. Understand the long-term consequences *for you* of thinking and behaving like a Two. This is the most important step in motivating your climb out of this stage. This means learning from your mistakes rather than inventing excuses for them, and resolving to walk down the

path that's consistent with your *long-term* goals. For example, consider showing genuine respect for some of the people who follow the very rules you may have fought up until now.

3. Get involved with something larger than yourself. Allow people to help you without exploiting them or jumping to the conclusion that they have an ulterior motive to con *you* in some way. These are the attitudes that will help you to begin developing empathy, which is simply an awareness of how other people feel and how you would feel if you were the object of the actions you are inflicting on others. You were undoubtedly taught the Golden Rule sometime in early childhood. Reconsider it as you work on your Stage Two hooks—especially the part that says "as you would have others do unto you." You will find many rewarding alternatives to your problematic Stage Two hooks as you read about the higher stages and begin to develop an internal sense of purpose and spirituality.

Perhaps as importantly, don't forget the wonderfully *positive* side of Stage Two, which is your most primal source of sheer joy, uninhibited play, and the self-permission to dispose of all unwanted inhibitions!

Most of us can manage our problematic Stage Two hooks once we recognize them. More than anything else, it's a matter of identifying and changing your self-defeating attitudes, many of which were listed earlier in this chapter.

Here are some affirmations you can use for managing your Stage Two hooks. Believing and adopting them is the key to defeating the problematic side of Stage Two:

- "Nobody has everything they want. This is an impossible standard."
- "Life is not always easy, and I choose to accept that."
- "There are long-term benefits *to me* in treating others as I would like to be treated."
- "Frustration and discomfort are a part of life that can lead to good things, if only I am open to this fact."
- "I can't usually control how people treat me, only my reaction to them."
- "When I react with anger and a desire for revenge, I only cause myself additional pain."
- "If I'm not treated well, I can choose not to take it personally."
- "There are ways to get what I want in my life and overcome challenges without taking advantage of others or bringing negative consequences to myself."
- "I can now genuinely value the people in my life—especially those who have been there for me."
- "I take responsibility and accept the consequences for my actions and behavior."
- "I now value things in my life that are larger then myself."

4. As you did with Stage One affirmations, pick the attitudes from the list above that speak to you the most. (You can find this complete exercise for all of the stages in the appendix.) Remind yourself of these Stage Two affirmations several times a day. Most importantly: *Consciously live by them until become hardwired, which is to say that they become automatic and second nature to you.*

Beliefs and attitudes are little more than habits of thinking. How long they take to change varies from person to person, but clinical experience shows that with real commitment, three to six weeks is about average for permanent change to occur.

5. Take some steps in the right direction. Climbing out of Stage Two is about learning limits that may have eluded you earlier in life. Where could you use more self-discipline in your life? How would your life be richer if you could be *without* your problematic Stage Two hooks?

6. Identify what you are *willing* to change about yourself—especially where the changes might not instantly feel gratifying, but could have long-term positive effects for you (such as finishing college). As with Stage One, at Stage Two, becoming aware of your hooks and making a commitment to do what it takes to change them is most of the battle.

Reflect on This Question:

7. Reflect on this question and answer it for yourself: *"Why must I always have what I want?"* Do you know of any actual person firsthand (celebrities or others you know only by hearsay don't count) who has everything he or she wants? I certainly don't know anyone like that and never have! How could your life be better if you just changed this one attitude?

At Stage Three—and beyond, of course—your view of the world becomes radically different.

CHAPTER FIVE

Stage Three
Living Life by Your Rules

Always let your conscience be your guide.
—JIMINY CRICKET

For reasons we'll discuss in this chapter, I've often found it rather daunting to deal with the Threes I've encountered, perhaps more so than with any of the other stages. That may be because at Stage Three it can be so natural to operate as though making your own choices were not an option. And much of my personal mission is to teach people how to empower themselves by recognizing and then living by the infinite array of choices available to them.

Stage Three is about examining the rules you live by. The challenge here is also to modify them, if necessary, to fit exactly with that unique passion and purpose-driven life you are committed to living.

*   *   *

Imagine living in a world where everything is exactly as it "should" be. In this world, rules rule. In other words, all rules are effortlessly obeyed, all authority figures are placated, all norms are satisfied, and you can easily stand up to the toughest scrutiny in any area of your life. The powers are making no demands whatsoever on you that you are not fully meeting.

Imagine that same standard is also being met by everyone who looks up to *you* as an authority. All rules you impose on others are being followed as well. This is not a glimpse of the Cold War–era Soviet Union or a scene out of George Orwell's frightening novel *Nineteen Eighty-Four*, but Stage Three at its very *best*. To fit in, you simply need to do, and perhaps believe, whatever the authorities expect you to. As a Three, that ability and willingness to *fit in and obey the rules* means that life is good!

The rest of childhood up until early adolescence is when Stage Three is most normal and age-appropriate. This is the best time to learn, understand, integrate, and fine-tune the many basic yet complex rules of living in our civilized society. At Stage Three, children rarely see themselves yet as unique or one-of-a-kind individuals, but are optimally moving in that direction. They seek and are most comfortable with solid structure, although at times their Stage Two hooks can make them seem as self-centered and egocentric as they were earlier in life.

Stage Three

Stage Three is the usual stage through late childhood, where it's important to learn the rules of living in a civilized society. Stage Three *problematic hooks* can morph us into various degrees of being rigid rule abiders...

+ Authoritarian personality.

+ Not yet ready to be unique.

+ Inflexible regarding rules and ideas.

 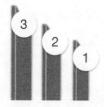

Stage Three is characterized by the desire to fit in and be part of a group so as to connect with and relate to peers. Also during this stage, conscience gradually develops, making you now capable of some empathy toward others—at least with respect to your impact on them.

The best parenting for a child at Stage Three provides a solid structure and resolve to do whatever it takes to learn the rules of life. When they are given loving guidance along with appropriate discipline, children have the best possible environment to learn what it takes not only to fit in, but to thrive and begin to discover their uniqueness.

At Stage Three, a child's world expands. People outside of home become important resources for the first time. Giving to others can now be a pleasurable experience. Peer friendships can be chosen, and a child's imagination begins to develop richly. The best possible scenario for developing hooks to the highest stages occurs when parents and teachers encourage and stimulate that imagination, causing creativity to expand and flourish throughout life. And there is no better time for children to begin to discover that it's desirable to listen to their inner voice. It is this source that will become a lifelong channel to uniqueness, creativity, and the motivation for taking charge of any aspect of life. At Stage Three, most children begin to develop many of their other hooks to the highest stages as well. For example, talent in such things as art, music, and sports begins to show up, as well as an awareness of giving back through charitable activities.

Primarily, Stage Three is about learning and accepting certain rules that protect our world, save lives, and teach about long-term consequences. Some are no-brainers: not to break things, injure ourselves, maim, murder, or rob people. It is our willingness to adhere to these and similar rules that makes our species unique and puts us above the primitive nature of Stage Two. Without our Stage Three nature, humankind probably would not have survived this long!

The lifelong Stage Three challenge, however, is not only to learn and understand the rules that apply to us and our world, but also to question them when they no longer make sense. For example, a hammer is a very useful tool, but it is also one with which you can hurt yourself. The

Stage Three

Stage Three is about examining the rules you live by.

The challenge here is to modify them, if necessary, to fit with your best passion and purpose-driven life.

mind is a tool as well, and just like a hammer, the mind has its downside. One misuse of the mind is to maintain many rules that simply do not continue to work or serve you, and then to manufacture even more rules, along with reasons why we as well as others must follow them. At the beginning of Stage Three, the mechanism for distinguishing, questioning, and disputing rules (as opposed to acting out against them) is barely developed, if at all. Ideally, this gradually changes.

In addition to parents and peers, teachers are also critical at Stage Three. Teachers are the professionals who are in a position to have the most important impact on children at Stage Three. The ones who meet this challenge leave indelible imprints on their students, and they make an immeasurable contribution to the world with their continuing influence throughout a student's later life. Sadly, many teachers do not fully rise to this crucial occasion. I refer here mainly to those who can teach such things as reading and math quite well, but are out of their league when it comes to encouraging creativity, critical thinking, people skills, and the benefits of being an individual.

Teachers may also operate as Threes in their careers. They often mistake their students' creativity for defiance rather than the Stage Six hook that creativity is for youngsters. At the extreme, repressive and punitive elementary-school teachers can not only shut down creativity, but also instill a hatred of learning, as well as a fear of daring to be different.

This happened to me early in elementary school, where some teachers tended to treat any perceived act of defiance harshly and dealt with it in as degrading and humiliating a manner as they could get away with. I had such a teacher when I was a child in the first grade. I remember watching a prison movie on TV and actually envying the prisoners because they didn't have to go to school. I came to think of it as a repressive environment, where teachers were to be feared and avoided. It wasn't until much later that I was able to change this view. Some good may have come from this experience in that I learned to challenge dogma at every turn and devote my career to helping others do so and thus live by their *chosen* rules.

Linda: "I could never understand that old adage that rules are made to be broken. To me, a rule was a rule—

Conflict

**Your *Ultimate Goal* at Stage Three:
to be conflict-free**

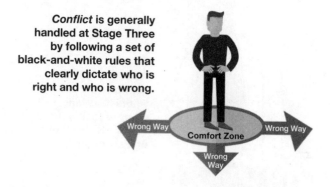

**Conflict is generally
handled at Stage Three
by following a set of
black-and-white rules that
clearly dictate who is
right and who is wrong.**

Wrong Way   Comfort Zone   Wrong Way

Wrong
Way

simple as that. Anyone I dated had to be perfect, so I didn't
date anyone very long until I met my husband, who seemed
to meet the standard. But once we were married, my many
rigidities took over, and this one rather strong hook de-
stroyed my first marriage." We will hear more later about
how Linda was affected by her Stage Three hooks. At this
point we can just note that her ultimate goal as a Three was
to be "conflict-free"—a standard that can come at a very
high price.

Obviously circumstances do not always support the
black-and-white thinking that underlies this Stage Three
notion. To the degree that an adult operates as a Three in an
area of life, he or she usually has much difficulty accepting
or tolerating exceptions to rules. An adult Three will characteristically tend to become something of an excessive con-
formist, a rigid rule abider, or an authoritarian personality,

Beware of your comfort zone or what I have long referred to as your "comfortable state of discomfort."

letting the fear of punishment, authority, and retribution dictate any—or at the extreme, even every—aspect of life.

Conflict is generally handled at Stage Three by following a set of black-and-white rules that "clearly dictate" who is right and who is wrong. Because challenging rules or authority is generally out of the question for them, Threes are often in a box. Closed to new ideas that question their deeply embedded rules, they seek people and situations that reinforce their conformity to certain beliefs, lifestyle choices, and ways to behave. When Threes find more comfort in the rigidities they have adopted than pain from being stifled by them, there's little reason or motivation to climb out of Stage Three. This comfort zone is what I have long called your *comfortable state of discomfort*. Think of it as an internal force to be reckoned with when deciding to climb out of any stage, but especially the first three.

Like most Stage Three attitudes, beliefs about gender roles, sexual behavior, making a living, and certain stereotypes tend to be quite rigid and are often defended with self-righteous anger. Prejudice, bigotry, and intolerance are also Stage Three hooks.

Samuel: "The television character Archie Bunker (who could be considered a Stage Three icon) could have headed the house I grew up in. We had a set of unbending rules we had to live by for everything: how to dress, what to eat, the religion and ethnic background of our friends and whom we dated. My parents wouldn't let us associate with kids whose parents had divorced or who were different in practically any way at all from us. It wasn't until I went to college that I realized how isolated we were and how many things existed that we were never allowed to even think about. I was a junior in college when I met my future wife. The idea that there is more than one option with respect to who stays home with the children versus who earns a living, and even what is acceptable to enjoy as a leisure-time activity, was at first downright frightening. But it opened my eyes to infinite possibilities, and I am quite thankful that it did. Getting my parents to accept my wife took some time, but they eventually realized that having a relationship with their grandchildren and me depended on it. Unbelievably, my siblings and I have even seen some cracks in their rigidity, leading me to believe that anyone can change their ways."

Most functional marriages and love relationships grounded in Stage Three are governed by dictums that neither partner challenges. When working with many couples over the years, I have observed that sometimes the partners in a sense become psychological clones of each other: they have exactly the same or very similar ideas and values about family, finances, politics, religion, sex, the roles of each partner and family member, child rearing, and virtually all of the major issues that are staples of most relationships. Usually they have not evaluated or chosen these rules but have adopted them uncritically, often from generation to generation. Disagreements typically focus on who's most compliant with the rules that form the basis of their relationship. When conflicts are settled, it is normally by this unwritten rule book as well.

A marriage or love relationship may not survive when one partner begins to climb out of Stage Three and challenges some of the basic assumptions by which the couple lives, while the other partner remains attached to his or her rigidities. Partners at any stage can and certainly do grow apart, but when they do it for this reason, look for that problematic Stage Three hook in one or both partners.

For Linda, the self-described rigid rule abider we met earlier in the chapter, her marriage ended after her husband decided, despite her objections, to accept a significant promotion that required him to be out of town one or two days a week. Her parents often boasted that in their thirty-five-year marriage they had never spent a day apart. Linda believed that this was the only way a marriage could be—with both parents there every single day, without exception, for the kids and each other. "For a long time, I blamed the divorce on my husband choosing his career over me," Linda said. "I now realize how rigid I was. We just couldn't handle conflict. If it hadn't been that, some other conflict—and we had many, with our sex life, how we handled money, how he related to my family—would have probably caused us to break up."

If I have learned one thing from working with thousands of couples, it's that the ability to handle conflict is perhaps the best indication of whether a relationship lasts. Couples who can resolve conflicts can use those skills with issues regarding finances, parenting, the roles of family and in-laws, religious differences, where to live, the use of leisure time, sex, and even infidelity.

It is at Stage Three that spiritual development begins. But here, like most other things at this stage, spirituality is usually another set of rules to follow without question. Most often they are the rules of an organized religion. They entail the belief that God will take care of you, but only if you unbendingly obey his commandments and the dictums of the religious organization to which you belong. If not, you incur God's wrath. For many, fundamentalist religious beliefs have great appeal in that little or nothing is left to question or interpret. If that works for you, it's certainly an example of a Stage Three hook you can choose to keep and cherish.

Julie: "When I was nineteen, I left what I thought was a really oppressive home environment, where my father's 'my way or the highway' attitude was unquestioned. It was suffocating, and I felt I was too old for it. My roommate at the time got me interested in attending the meetings of a spiritual community, which I then thought would give me something I needed. But it meant that I got very involved with, then hooked by, a cult that was even more tyrannical than the home I'd left, only I didn't realize it at the time! Their approach was to lure you in until you felt they were the wonderful and loving family you never had. Once you fit in, they used guilt and fear to indoctrinate you and keep you isolated and totally committed to them. There were unbending not-to-be-questioned rules and pat 'solutions' to virtually all of your problems and questions about life. There were no inner conflicts, as long as you were a follower. When after five years I finally broke free, I felt like I'd gotten out of a concentration camp. Now that I know what spirituality actually is, I realize that there was nothing spiritual about it. At last I feel free to grow up."

Cults are often a type of rogue religion that usually benefits the charismatic leader more than anyone else. Nevertheless, religion and spirituality are two entirely different things, although legitimate religions can offer highly spiritual experiences for most people. I define spirituality as something *personal and distinctive* that is *internal* and within each of us. Spiritually is connected to our higher self, whatever form that takes, as well as our unique calling or life purpose. Yet most organized religions emphasize how humans are the same as opposed to how we are unique.

When religion is a choice that helps connect you to your higher self and the distinct life you were born to live, it is certainly the pathway to your true spirituality. On the other hand, religion by itself is an *externally* organized set of beliefs that defines spiritual things as well as how life is and is not to be lived. Threes often turn to the church for help when trying to resolve inner conflicts (e.g., anxiety, depression, or guilt) or relationship or marital issues (such as deciding whether to stay together or about sexual matters). It is at Stage Three where predetermined beliefs as explained by the Bible and clergy are probably the most comforting.

The old cliché that says "Never argue about religion or politics" is clearly grounded in Stage Three. These are two areas where rigid Stage Three hooks will rarely allow enough flexibility to recognize that there could be any valid alternative point of view at all.

In Stage Three–oriented families and social circles, age and position (such as being a patriarch or matriarch) grants authority automatically, as opposed to authority and respect being earned. (Interestingly, across all stages, the best predictor of a person's career choice seems to be the field of his or her most influential parent.)

George: "For years, I was considered the black sheep of the family. My sin? I had no interest in joining the family business, which was a lucrative career track for my siblings and their spouses as well as my father and uncles. It wasn't until I married, had children, and achieved success in my own career path that I felt somewhat—but not completely—accepted again. But my own *self*-acceptance improved greatly once I understood how this family rule made it necessary for me to choose between conforming and having a life I didn't want and having the life I truly wanted. All I can say now is 'What a no-brainer!'"

In addition to the absence of conflict, Threes typically define happiness as the familiarity and the safety of fitting in with those most like them. They also like to maintain the status quo and remain conflict-free by predictably choosing to be what they "should be" as opposed to what they *could* be. I don't know whether George's siblings chose the family business for these reasons or out of a true and healthy passion for it. But I've worked with many people and helped them clear Stage Three hooks so that, like George, they could make choices based on desire instead of fear.

Here is a sampling of some of the most common attitudes and beliefs you could have about yourself that may be powering your problematic Stage Three hooks and keeping you stuck. See which, if any, of these you recognize as helping to define one or more parts of your life:

- "I must fit in by doing only what I should do and by being what I should be—what's expected of me—or some dire consequence will result."
- "Others must do things my way."
- "Others must believe the same things I do."
- "The only way to avoid conflict is to follow strict tradition and obey the rules exactly."
- "I've had certain beliefs and attitudes as long as I can remember. Even if they no longer serve me, changing them will lead to more chaos and conflict in my life than I can handle."
- "Without a tight, rigid, and predictable structure, I can't manage my life."
- "It's always wrong to question authority."
- "There's no such thing as a good reason to break the law or disobey a rule, and those who do should always be punished severely."

Take a moment to identify and customize your own variations on these Stage Three themes. If any of them speak to you, decide which of them you're committed to changing. How have they affected your relationships, your career, and other essential areas of your life? How could your life improve if you could be free of them, that is, could convert them to choices that are at your disposal, instead of having these internalized rules rule you?

June: "For a long time I was content with my life simply because I believed there was no other alternative. I'd become programmed over time to automatically give in to my anxiety. In other words, my life was about not leaving my comfort zone. The problem was that as time went on, I felt trapped, and this depressed me, while attempting to do anything about it made me anxious. So I was constantly caught between the depression and anxiety until I understood that this was a situation I created and could therefore change. That gave me the courage to face my fears and pursue dreams that would have been previously unthinkable."

Mary: "The strongest, most comfortable, and most passionate relationship I'd ever had was with a man who had been divorced. I had a rule that said I could never marry someone with that in his background. So we broke up, and I settled for marrying someone who on paper was acceptable. But our marriage lasted only a little over a year. Then I was damaged goods as well. Fortunately, I got the epiphany that my rigidity was what ruined the relationship I really wanted. It's a long story, but I got a second chance with the love of my life, and I am now happily married to him. Best of all, I learned that some rules that were once very comforting no longer work, and that I now have the power to determine this and make my own choices!"

In my practice, I have observed that those who seek help for Stage Three–related issues normally do so when the book of rules that they have been living by no longer provides them with solace or solutions. Situations such as an illness, a severe loss, a spouse having an affair or leaving, the rebellion of an older child, or a need to cope with some other involuntary change of circumstances can be wake-up calls. Sometimes a first step in working through these issues is to look for an exception or contradiction in your own rule book. This can act almost as permission for beginning the climb out of Stage Three. In June's case, her anxiety and depression motivated her to begin to make some necessary changes. Once she started and knew that she could take charge of her life, she saw things in an entirely different way. Then there was no stopping her!

One definition of success at Stage Three is the ability to remain on the good side of anyone in authority. Authoritarianism is the Stage Three definition of authority. In totalitarian countries, run by a dictator who rules by fear and oppression, being compliant is necessary for survival. In more familiar contexts, authority figures need not have earned the *authoritative* quality required by those in the higher stages. They just have to be individuals you choose to follow by virtue of their role and your fear of defying them. A physician or an attorney, for example, or others with certain credentials may also be seen at Stage Three as someone not to be questioned.

Bosses in the workplace who operate from Stage Three characteristically use fear and intimidation to manage their subordinates with a "my way or the highway" attitude. Quite often in authoritarian organizations, Stage Three bosses experience their own superiors in the same way, never questioning someone of a higher position or rank. Many organizations (such as the military, post office, police and fire departments, and large construction or factory-type operations) deliberately and often rightly perceive this form of unbending, by-the-book management as necessary for accomplishing their mission. Thus a Stage Three management style does have its place, but for maximum effectiveness, it's a rather limited one.

Threes have the most fun when doing the "right" fun activities exactly as they "should" be doing them—that is, by a combination of fitting in and feeling the support of whatever authority they perceive (correctly or incorrectly) as looking over their shoulder. An environment for fun and play may be one that is safe and has a clear structure and unambiguous rules. Threes have a definite awareness of other people, and can usually relate well to members of their "tribe" who conform, have lots in common with them, possess similar beliefs and attitudes, and, most importantly, share the same values and follow the same rules. An easy definition of those who are most content at Stage Three would be *happy conformists*. They live their lives transparently and by the book, until they break free of what is often a stifling fear of their own uniqueness.

Climbing out of Stage Three: What You Need to Know

Once you recognize that there is a better way to live, the good news is that the process of moving beyond this stage is a simple one. It's about awakening to new ideas and pursuing them. The first step is to make the choice and commitment to identify and dismantle your problematic Stage Three hooks. *Often the simple awareness of a Stage Three hook is all that's necessary for quickly moving beyond it.* Next, take a risk or two that undermines these obsolete rules and beliefs. This is the simple part. However, *simple* is not the same as *easy*, and what may not be easy is the realization that you no longer fit in as effortlessly with certain friends, associates, and family members. Simply remembering that you actually have your newly discovered power can also be a challenge until it becomes second nature.

Look for alternative ways to both see and resolve conflicts. Dare to be different! Regardless of the area of life—work, marriage, friendships—be open to new ideas and other points of view. Go out of your way to accept others who are different from you. Work hard at understanding—which is not necessarily the same as agreeing with—their point of view and accept that many other alternatives exist, which may be just as valid for someone else as yours are for you. Most likely you already do this in certain areas of your life. Now is the time to let yourself enjoy broadening your horizons even further!

Stage Three Memo

You can now:
Get out of your comfort zone.
Make your own rules.
Create your own life and lifestyle.
Live by your own values.

Now for those attitudes that are most helpful for climbing out of Stage Three. See which of these you now need to hardwire the most:

- "I am ready to start examining the unquestioned rules I have lived by."
- "I am ready to start examining the rules that I have demanded others live by."
- "I am ready to be more flexible and open to new ideas that are now a better fit for me and my life. I discard those that do not work for me any longer."
- "Fitting in is only one of many choices that are now available to me. I am capable of considering all of the possibilities available to me."
- "Leaving my comfort zone may seem scary at first, but the discomfort that comes with new things is only temporary. It's well worth the permanent benefits of expanding my world."

- "It's OK to feel, think, and act differently than I am used to, and I can accept others who feel, think, and act differently than I do. I can now tolerate conflict or ambivalence when it arises."
- "Things are rarely black and white. In the real world, most things can be more accurately characterized by shades of gray."
- "I now accept flexibility and uncertainty without fearing dire consequences."

1. As you did those with the affirmations in the two previous stages, pick the attitudes from the list above that speak to you the most. Customize your affirmations to fit your situation exactly, and make them specific to your Stage Three hooks. You will find this exercise as it applies to all the stages in the appendix.

2. Examine what you have always wanted to do with your life but have resisted because you were afraid to leave behind that comfortable state of discomfort. If many things come to mind, make a complete list of them all. What are the risks you wish you could take now?

3. Ask yourself what steps you are willing to take in order to pursue what you really want now, even though it may mean being different or taking a path that leads you out of your comfort zone.

Climbing Out of Stage Three

Make the choice and commitment to identify and dismantle your problematic Stage Three hooks.

Next, take a risk or two that undermines whatever obsolete rules and beliefs you realize you'd be better off without.

Look for alternative ways to both see and resolve conflicts. *Be open to new ideas* **and other points of view.**

Old Way

Comfort Zone

New Alternative

New Possibilities

Dare to be different.

4. Next, make a commitment to begin taking some of these risks you have identified—perhaps very small ones at first, working your way up to the more important ones. Do whatever it takes to make you more comfortable leaving your comfort zone and to move you closer to your unique desires.

If living a fulfilling life at your highest potential is the product of the choices you make, then the more and wider range of choices you have, the better. This is the greatest benefit of dismantling your Stage Three hooks. *Entering the zone of your highest potential requires that you march to the sound of your own drum!* Don't insist on acceptance of your higher-stage behavior from old friends and family members who are still operating at lower stages. They may or may not ever understand you. But now you can certainly choose to understand them. Even so, sometimes you will forget that they cannot relate to certain things about you as you evolve. Preserving valuable relationships often means giving those people a pass and accepting the stubborn reality that they are doing the best they can.

On the other hand, be mindful of how you react to people who negate your right to have a point of view different from theirs. What you say and how you relate to them is not nearly as important as how you feel *within yourself* when they try to make you feel wrong. You have the power to determine the importance of anyone in your life and how much influence they might have on your beliefs, attitudes, and behaviors. Climbing out of Stage Three is about honoring your own personal power!

Make a special effort to look more to what people *do* rather than to what they say or to the title, position, or rank they hold. Moreover, if you tend to judge people by the groups they belong to (e.g., ethnic, racial, political, ideological, economic, age, religion, sex, sexual orientation), resolve to look beyond those factors and to the individual instead. Whenever you do this, you are indeed moving beyond Stage Three.

You, like everyone else on this planet, are different from any other human being ever created since the beginning of time. Moreover, there will never be another exactly like you. Do something new each day to honor rather than fight or ignore this wonderful reality!

At Stage Four, anxieties may surface, but our unique identities unfold.

CHAPTER SIX

Stage Four
Becoming Fearless

The only thing we have to fear is fear itself.
—Franklin Delano Roosevelt

FDR's most recognized quote is actually a paraphrase of something that has been said by many notables throughout history. It's also the most important statement that you need to remember about virtually all of your Stage Four hooks.

It's now time to obliterate our fears and anxieties, along with their consequences, as Stage Four hooks can block access to your reservoir of courage that you need to be unique. If anxiety, perfectionism, insecurity, the tendency to put yourself down, or fear of failure or rejection is holding you back, then this is an important chapter for you. Let's trade those fears and anxieties for self-confidence and courage!

**Imagine yourself being as famous
as you could ever want to be...**

Receiving unconditional admiration and being
wildly applauded—even routinely receiving
standing ovations just for showing up!

But first, let's look at an appealing Stage Four image. Imagine yourself being as famous as you could ever want to be, receiving unconditional admiration, and being wildly applauded—even receiving standing ovations just for showing up. This level of admiration might come from those who are closest or most important to you, such as your family, friends, those in your workplace, or neighbors, or perhaps even by crowds of adoring strangers, the way celebrities experience it.

Being liked and admired by your social circle or by others around you; being a highly popular and respected luminary in your field, with a showcase full of awards; and being a celebrity are just a few examples of appealing aspirations powered by Stage Four hooks. And who wouldn't be tempted by these images? However, it's important to explore how much energy you're expending to seek these goals and how your efforts may or may not be benefiting you. So reflect for a moment on what you do to achieve the approval and admiration of others and whether your efforts actually get you what you want. What price do you pay when, for example, you say you agree with something just to be agreeable when in fact you disagree?

And while we're on the subject, how much money do you spend that you may not even have to buy things you don't really need to impress people that you may not even like? Sure, the thrills that Fours seek are always possible for you to experience *as fantasies*—and you certainly don't have to be Walter Mitty to imagine them. But what price do you pay in your life to strive for that admiration and recognition? How much approval by others do you tell yourself you need? What do you fear about not having it? And what are you willing to do to avoid the consequences of not getting it? You may want to take a moment to ponder these questions.

Here is another Stage Four challenge: Never judge yourself negatively about your Stage Four hooks. Instead, be mindful of them and resolve to accept *yourself* at least as much as you want other people to accept you.

At Stage Three, you are naturally drawn to rules and "shoulds" by which to live your life. When you remain

Some Common Stage Four Images

 Being *universally* well liked and admired by your social circle or others around you

 Being a highly popular and respected luminary in your field

 Being a celebrity

attached to those rules when they no longer apply, you do so either out of habit or in exchange for a feeling of security. At Stage Four, many of those rules no longer give you the emotional support they once did. Thus you now find it natural to start questioning old dictums and exploring new choices. While breaking out of the pack is desirable and often feels liberating, it also raises some new issues, such as anxiety about being accepted—which was not a major dilemma when you unquestioningly conformed at Stage Three.

Your self-consciousness at this stage triggers fears of such things as rejection, looking foolish, failure, and isolation. These anxieties are the forces that both create and power your Stage Four hooks. The preoccupation with love and approval from others and the need to be, or at least seem to be, perfect, are common examples of challenges at Stage Four.

Here's a simple fact that's often lost on those who operate out of Stage Four: *what other people think of you is*

Fact

What other people think of you is really none of your business! ⟶ **And very much out of your control.**

What People Think of You

none of your business! Furthermore, somebody else's opinion of you is one of those things you can least control or even know about. Some people will like you because they see you as docile or inferior to them in some way. Others could hate you because they believe you are more successful or attractive than they are. Still others could like you for the very reason someone else dislikes you! For example, in the workplace, many of the hardest workers experience scorn or rejection from the others, who resent having to live up to the higher standards these hard workers set. Yet I would hardly be inclined to advise anyone to lower their standards merely to be liked by coworkers who want to pull them in the direction of mediocrity. There's no guarantee that this would win their approval anyway. Yes, pleasing and impressing others and being recognized, honored, and ac-

Stage Four

Stage Four is the stage throughout adolescence when we ideally come to accept ourselves for the unique individuals we've become. Our *problematic* Stage Four hooks often result in a wide variety of self-defeating behavior...

+ Approval seeking
+ Anxiety and depression
+ Self-doubt and shame
+ Perfectionism
+ Fear of failure or success
+ Self-consciousness

Much like the most difficult aspects of our adolescence.

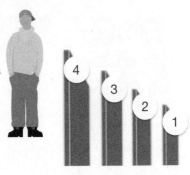

cepted are things most of us strive for at times. However, for Fours, these issues can be all-consuming and can exact a very high cost.

Stage Four is the normal stage of development during adolescence up and until early adulthood—from the ages of approximately eleven or twelve to twenty-one. *The psychological mission of adolescence is ideally to become secure enough within yourself to establish your solid identity as a unique individual.* That uniqueness is a major ingredient for your foundation as a mature adult. Under the best of circumstances, you will build upon this trait for the rest of your life. Typically, adolescents can be obsessed with peer approval, fitting in with groups they select, learning how to make themselves attractive to those they wish to attract, and, most importantly, gaining self-acceptance. The best parenting of adolescents who are navigating Stage Four is keenly sensitive to the unique needs and challenges common to this developmental period.

Naturally a ready-made conflict develops between being a unique individual and conforming to those around you. Much of the Stage Four conflict, like adolescence itself, is about determining whether to go with what is expected of you—as in Stage Three—or to go your own way. The latter course will sometimes work for you and lead you to good things. Other times it may not and will bring you back to familiar and deeply embedded Stage Three–type rules. However, as a Four, whether and when you follow those rules is your choice. This ongoing dance continues throughout adolescence, until you figure out the right mix for you and you alone. This is the signal that you are ready to leave Stage Four and embrace early adulthood.

Early love relationships are an important part of the adolescent ritual. It's been said that a sane human being goes through something akin to insanity under only two circumstances in life: during adolescence and when falling in love. Curiously, both of these are Stage Four challenges!

Even so, as with your hooks at all stages, if your Stage Four hooks are enhancing your life, enjoy them. For example, when in love, your Stage Four hooks can sometimes add to those delicious romantic feelings of unconditional love and extreme well-being. When this is at a fever pitch, life rarely feels better. Of course, be mindful of your expectations, as this "dopamine high" phase of a relationship rarely lasts as long as we wish it would.

Dorothy: "I was so addicted to the buzz of a new romance that when that bliss quieted down, I immediately assumed that it was time to move on. I was obsessed with how much I was being loved. It wasn't until I could see through this illusion that I was able to make a long-term relationship work." A bit later we'll revisit Dorothy's challenge and what she needed to do in order to have the relationship she wanted.

Stage Four hooks make for good choices in other circumstances as well. A bit of anxiety can be a good thing sometimes. It can help keep you on your toes in situations where peak performance is important. That's why many professional performers talk about an optimal degree of anxiety that gives their performance a positive edge. You may have noticed that same phenomenon when on a job interview, making a presentation, or taking an important exam. Using salesmanship skills to impress others or to make a top-notch appearance as part of a larger goal is also a function of Stage Four at its best.

Never confuse anxiety with fear, even though they often feel the same. Fear can navigate you through a truly dangerous situation. It can be a life-saving emotion when it's used to help ensure your physical survival. When there is an actual danger, fear can both alert you and arm your body to fight or flee most efficiently. No matter how far

You're Using Positive Stage Four Hooks . . .

When enjoying the "buzz" or bliss of being "in love" or adored in a new romance.

When selling yourself where the image you put out to others is important.

When it's your desire to fit into a chosen group where peer approval is required.

When an optimal degree of anxiety can be a good thing sometimes for performances.

beyond Stage Four you have climbed, you will still have access to that channel if you ever need it. Anxiety can also be about worry, or pretending that a danger exists when it really doesn't. And most anxiety is indeed stifling. Yet even anxiety or worry can be beneficial when it acts as a wake-up call to alert you to a situation that cries out for attention.

Your problematic Stage Four hooks produce anxiety, self-doubt, and other forms of insecurity. Until dismantled, they can be the forces behind your biggest and most difficult life challenges. As a psychotherapist, I probably spend as much time helping clients with their hooks in Stage Four as on all of the other lower stages combined. This pervasiveness is partly what makes this stage so important to understand and work through.

James: "For as long as I could remember, I let what I feared were other people's opinions of me torment me: those of my siblings, teachers, friends, coworkers, neighbors, eventually my children, and virtually anyone else in my orbit. I clearly put my own self-esteem in the hands of everyone else. I needed people to admire me and craved approval so much that it was my main motivator."

Mark: "Despite being gay, I married a woman in order to blend in, until I could no longer live this lie. When I finally came out and my marriage ended, most of the important friends, family, and colleagues in my life that I was sure would reject me because of this were either supportive or made it clear that it was no big deal. Once the shock wore off, even my ex-wife was relieved to get an explanation for my sexual unresponsiveness, which was understandably very frustrating for her." Mark came to realize that the people who count are rarely as judgmental of you as you think they are, or as you are of yourself. I have observed this to be a life-changing epiphany for many people.

As adults, our Stage Four hooks take us back to many of the themes and challenges of adolescence. For example, adolescence is the ideal time to learn how to handle conflict, since making mistakes then is normally far less consequential than it will be later in life. (Perhaps that's why in many ways conflict is the norm at Stage Four.) For example, if public speaking makes you nervous, think of how your anxiety about giving a speech might be a metaphor for how you handle conflict. There is a conflict between the desire to speak despite the anxiety and letting your anxiety rule by avoiding the speech. Your desire to attain a larger goal is telling you to speak, and the anxiety is saying not to.

Public speaking usually turns up high on the list—often in first place—when surveys are done of what people fear the most. Public-speaking anxiety is just a Stage Four hook. Your fear of speaking to a group is really anxiety and self-consciousness about rejection, ridicule, or negative judgment by those who hear you speak. If you let your anxiety win, you could convince yourself to avoid these situations altogether, at the expense of a higher goal or a reward for making the speech. The same is true for other varieties of performance anxiety as well—whether triggered by taking a job interview or connected with sexual performance. Fours characteristically handle conflict by taking the road that produces the least anxiety *in the moment*. If you allow your anxiety to determine whether you face a conflict or avoid it, you might avoid certain challenges that, if successfully met, could result in an important accomplishment, a major success, or even a life-changing breakthrough.

Fours also tend to obsess about what they can do to be *seen by others* as successful. (Think of the biggest braggarts you know.) At Stage Four, anxieties about failing can cut very deeply into how you see yourself. A failed marriage, a financial setback, a lost job, or the inability to reach an important goal all can cause you to overreact—as would be typical in adolescence—by labeling yourself as a complete failure. Berating yourself in this global way can begin a vicious cycle that impairs both your self-image and your willingness to get back into the ring and try again.

Validation and acceptance by peers are extremely important at Stage Four. Adolescents often reluctantly find themselves using drugs, getting tattoos, or participating in certain sexual activities merely for acceptance, as opposed to fulfilling their own desires. Self-esteem issues are usually Stage Four hooks. In the best of all worlds, you will have established a foundation of self-confidence to build upon by early adolescence. But at Stage Four, how you perceive what others think of you can powerfully influence what you think of yourself: when you feel discounted or put down by detractors, it's common to think less of yourself as well. In the extreme, Stage Four hooks can cause self-doubt to become a way of life.

Happiness at Stage Four is belonging and feeling liked, loved, honored, or at least accepted by those you value the most. For celebrities who take themselves too seriously, the general public is part of that Stage Four network. A more realistic view for celebrities would be to enjoy the praise, recognition, and fuss when it's there, while realizing that it's not personal and will most likely fade when their fifteen minutes of fame is over.

Wanting to be an actor in order to be famous, admired, and envied (a popular Stage Four fantasy), as opposed to wanting to act because it is your talent, art and passion, is an example of Stage Four thinking.

Jana: "I became a teacher because I was attracted to the stature and power it seemed to provide. But I did not at all enjoy the actual day-to-day work. I soon quit being an art teacher, which felt repetitious and too structured, to pursue a career in commercial art, which allows me to do exactly what I love doing all day. I guess I had to get this prestige thing out of my system first."

I have also seen doctors and lawyers in my practice who disliked the work they did but admitted they were there because of their professions' prestige and the acceptance they perceived from their parents and others. In fact, I once coined the lighthearted term *beaholic* to describe this all-too-common Stage Four trait, in which individuals are focused on their titles and the image it exudes while not wanting to live up to the actual responsibilities of their roles.

Parents and others who provide guidance to children would be doing kids a big favor by asking them not "What do you want to *be* when you grow up?" but "What do you want to *do* when you grow up?"

In the workplace, Fours tend to be more concerned about how their accomplishments affect their own self-esteem than about the impact those contributions might have to the larger world.

Like Twos, Fours will sometimes "be whatever they have to be" to gain acceptance or respect. When Fours lie or mislead, they characteristically do so to impress others (unlike Twos, who lie to deceive, avoid punishment, or acquire personal gain). Fours often go out of their way to seek prestige and fame. They love to feel popular and superior, even if they realize deep down that this is merely an illusion or a fleeting state.

In Stage Four, as Stage Three, religion is sometimes a remedy for conflict and insecurity. But at Stage Four, the purpose of religion is not to avoid "punishment" but to get something positive. Sometimes prayer and meditation prove to be excellent antidotes for anxiety. At times this might be merely the result of the relaxation that meditation and prayer provide. On the other hand, at this stage there is now the capacity to reach for the deeper purpose achieved by handing your problems over to a loving and benevolent God or higher power. In addition, religious organizations often provide a much-needed community that provides genuine acceptance.

At Stage Four, you are not yet in command of your life. You're still a passenger, not the driver. This can certainly cause a great deal of suffering: worry over appearances; feeling bad about things that are unimportant in the grand scheme of life; or perhaps turning your own anger at something or someone inward and toward yourself.

Stage Four hooks can also take a toll on your marriage or love relationship. Insecurity issues, such as extreme jealousy, the constant questioning of and obsessing about how much your partner loves you, and sexual performance anxiety can often overpower the positives.

Jill: "In my twenties, I had a series of relationships that amounted to little more than an alternative to loneliness and the insecurities of being single rather than a real desire for the other person. But even when they weren't fulfilling for me, I was too insecure to move on. Instead I'd go out of my way to be a chronic pleaser, rather than confronting the troublesome issues head-on, which could upset the apple cart. When I was finally filled with resentment because I got nothing back, I'd leave, but only to repeat the pattern—that is, until I was able to come to grips with my own insecurities and expectations. Now I am finally in a healthy relationship."

Surprisingly, many relationships between Fours can do very well when both partners' issues are complementary, making them able to thrive together. Most romance novels, as well as just about every MGM musical, contain at least one Stage Four story line, such as jealousy or unrequited love. Fortunately, when both partners relate to each other at Stage Four and one begins to climb to a higher stage, the other may also be open to trying new attitudes, behaviors, and changes that could lead to growth both individually and as a couple. This degree of flexibility is rarely possible in the first three stages.

Now let's look at what powers this anxiety and insecurity as well as other problematic Stage Four hooks. As we did with the other stages, here are some of the attitudes and beliefs about yourself that could wreak havoc for you in any part of your life. See which of them apply to you:

- "What others think of me is crucially important, regardless of who they are or how I feel about them."
- "Impressing others is a necessity for me."
- "I *must* be loved or approved of by others and meet their expectations."
- "I can only accept myself to the degree that I am accepted by others."
- "I must do whatever it takes to be accepted in order to feel good about myself, because rejection is unbearable."
- "Failing at something [a relationship, a job, an exam, sexual performance, a goal] makes me a total failure to myself, in the eyes of others, or both."
- "Any result less than perfection is totally unacceptable."
- "_____ [fill in the name of someone specific] must love me in the exact way I require for our relationship to work. If not, our relationship is unfulfilling and perhaps even untenable."

Now identify, customize, and make a list of your own variations on these Stage Four themes. How have they affected your relationships, your career, and other essential areas of your life? How would your life improve if you could be free of them or convert them to choices? Make it a priority to decide which of these beliefs you're committed to changing.

Here's another important thing to remember: No matter how evolved you may be, Stage Four hooks can be present in almost any aspect of life. In fact, an adult without *some* Stage Four hooks could be the rarest human specimen there is!

Climbing out of Stage Four:
What You Need to Know to Overcome Anxiety and the Other Insecurities behind Your Problematic Hooks

The climb out of Stage Four simply challenges you to face down and let go of unnecessary anxieties and insecurities. Think of them as excess baggage you don't need. Personally, I have experienced more internal freedom to develop, create, and present new ideas since I gave up the need for others to view my work favorably. My relationships also became richer and more fulfilling once I let go of concerns about judgment or rejection. So I can't urge you enough to make a commitment to dismantle your problematic hooks.

They are diminishing the quality of your life simply by causing you to fear things that present no real danger.

The two main ingredients for your climb to higher stages are the *self-confidence* to succeed and unconditional *self-acceptance*, which means accepting yourself even when you're not successful. These are attitudes that you can choose to adopt right now.

Facing situations that trigger your anxiety head-on—and you know what they are—feels great after you have done it. It's also the definition of success in gaining control of your life when Stage Four hooks are holding you back. As you do, you will discover that taking risks that, at the very worst, could result in mere rejection or failure is indeed a no-lose proposition. If the idea of asking someone for a date or making a presentation triggers anxiety in you, do it anyway. If you succeed, then taking this kind of risk the next time will be a bit easier. That's a no-brainer. But even if your risk results in that dreaded failure or rejection, you win anyway! In this case, you win by knowing you had the courage to try it and then learning that you really can handle rejection and that, unpleasant as it may be, you *will* survive it! On the other hand, never taking the risk *guarantees* that you will not get what you want. Once you take the action to learn this experientially, you will be on the fast track to losing many or all of your fears of failure or rejection, regardless of how strong they may have been at their peak.

Sometimes asserting yourself involves overriding your fear of rejection in another way—by simply saying no to some request that you don't want to fulfill, rather than complying and feeling resentful afterwards. As Mark Twain said, "At the end of your life you will be more disappointed by the things you didn't do [and I'll add *say*] than by the ones you did." How true!

Now, let's look at the attitudes beliefs that you can choose, to dismantle your problematic Stage Four hooks:

- "People who don't accept me are rarely worth my time and attention."
- "Love and approval from certain people may be nice, but are not essential."
- "I will no longer put energy into trying to make others admire, envy, or love me. In reality, I can't control how anyone else feels about me."
- "I can certainly *choose* to impress someone, but I don't *need* to impress anybody."
- "I give myself unconditional acceptance regardless of who else does or does not."
- "I can only do my best, and I hereby let go of all versions of that impossible standard called perfection. Nothing and nobody can always be prefect."
- "Failing at something does *not* make me a failure."
- "I *can* handle rejection. In fact, each time I do, I am stronger for it."

1. As you did with the affirmations in the three previous stages, pick the ones from the list above that speak to you the most. Once again, customize them to fit your situation exactly, then write them down and put them into your smartphone or anywhere else you can easily access them. Most importantly, do what it takes to consciously live by them until they become hardwired. See the exercise in the appendix.

2. If challenging your Stage Four hooks seems too daunting, ask yourself, "What is the *worst* possible thing that could happen if what I feared the most (for example, a rejection by someone you are trying to impress) actually became a reality? Are the consequences really so dire that I need to continue living my life in deference to that fear?" If the answer is yes, then ask yourself why. Do not give up challenging these beliefs you have until you are satisfied that you are acting out of choice and courage rather than unwarranted fear or anxiety. If I had to pick one exercise that I do habitually—without even thinking about it— whenever an anxiety, a worry, or a concern comes up, it's this one. Please write it down and use it often. Nothing can expose a needless fear for what it is better and more easily than this simple technique.

Many families and peer groups unwittingly provide a breeding ground for avoidance and low self-confidence by promoting the "safe haven" of the status quo. When this happens, your hooks can feel even more daunting. Getting the help you need outside of your familiar circles is often the most important step. Psychotherapy, personal coaching, and group peer support, along with self-help techniques, are the best forms of intervention for climbing out of Stage Four.

Anxiety can sometimes feel too intense to permit the risk-taking and self-assertion that are necessary to defeat it. Therefore strategies designed to directly zero in on the anxiety can have wide ripple effects that will positively influence every aspect of your life. Anxiety is the only disease I know of whose cure is to ignore it. So make it a mission to confront each situation that makes you anxious, as well as those beliefs and attitudes that keep your anxieties in place.

If the world is a classroom, psychotherapy is tutoring. There are many excellent and well-proven therapeutic interventions for anxiety, anger, depression, phobias, and the conditions related to them. Never hesitate to get professional help in order to learn skills that you have not been able to master in the classroom of life. This includes skills in conflict resolution, coping with stress and anxiety, and assertiveness training. Life is full of conflicts. But there is *always* an alternative to letting conflicts defeat you.

Often we fear what we do not understand. It is therefore important to learn as much as you can about every

Stage Four Memo

Courage is simply an attitude that I can choose!

one of your hooks. For example, how have others successfully handled the challenges you are facing? There are now books, articles, websites, blogs and audio materials that deal with virtually every issue in existence.

3. Imagine for a moment that you are absolutely fearless, full of courage, and immune to anxiety. Say you no longer fear rejection from others, the prospect of looking foolish, or even publicly failing at something you consider important. What would you do differently? What life changes would you make that your fears or anxieties currently put beyond your reach? Make a list of whatever comes up for you, along with an idea or two for a strategy to take at least one *prudent* risk to counter each fear you listed. Example include researching a job change you want to make, asking your boss for a raise, asking someone out for a date, joining a social group, or bringing up

a difficult issue that you've been avoiding with a friend or your spouse.

If the fear of failure is rearing its ugly head, let me offer you my strongest view of what distinguishes a successful person from one who is unsuccessful. A successful person is someone who failed, used the failure as a learning experience, and tried again with the resulting new insight. An unsuccessful person is someone who failed and gave up. Successful people use failure as their most valuable sources of insight and wisdom for going forward, while unsuccessful people use failure as a reason to put themselves down and then, by default, let someone else be the one who achieves. As always, the choice is yours!

4. Act as if you were fearless. Consciously walk and even breathe as though you were fearless and full of courage. Try spending an hour at first, and work your way up to an entire day doing this. First, try it at a time when there is not much going on, for example, during a weekend or a day off that you can spend alone. Notice what comes up for you. Gradually extend this new mind-set to the times when it would matter most, such as during the week—perhaps to handle a dreaded but necessary work confrontation. The more comfortable you are with this attitude, the easier it becomes to act fearlessly. Great performers such as Sir Laurence Olivier often had stage fright but knew how to act as if they were in complete control. Soon the jitters would

disappear, meaning that they "fooled" themselves along with everyone else about their self-confidence!

Stage Four fantasies can be compelling and can seem desirable. If you crave adoration from others, your challenge is to determine consciously just how much of your life you are willing to devote to this goal and at what cost. Remember also that the approval you seek may not be possible for you to get, no matter what you do. Few people would disagree that it's nice to be loved or adored, approved of, and accepted by others. But in reality, it's rarely essential. So if this has been an issue for you, merely changing your expectations in the area of seeking approval can change your life profoundly. The best part is that from now on you can give yourself at least as much acceptance and approval as you seek from others. Then what somebody else thinks of you will never again take on more importance than it deserves.

*   *   *

At Stage Five, handling the balance of our life roles takes center stage.

CHAPTER SEVEN

Stage Five
Taking Charge of Your Life

Be open to everything, but attached to nothing.
—THE BUDDHA

"Am I normal?" Like most mental-health professionals, I am asked that question often, and in every context imaginable. As a psychological term, *being normal* has many definitions: average, typical, ordinary, balanced, free of certain symptoms, within the bell curve, and—the one that most people want to hear—*not crazy*. In the Stage Climbing process, the definition is simply Stage Five.

Stage Five is our default position for keeping our lives functioning, sane, together, and for the most part problem-free. As late adolescence morphs into early adulthood, we gradually begin to operate more and more in this stage. One of the main challenges for adults in our society is to be firmly in charge of all their many life roles without being overwhelmed by them. At Stage Five, this is an important definition of winning. But for reasons we'll explore in

Am I Normal?

"Being normal" has many definitions

- Average
- Typical
- Ordinary
- Balanced
- Within the "bell-shaped curve"
- An absence of certain symptoms
- *Not crazy*
- Stage Five

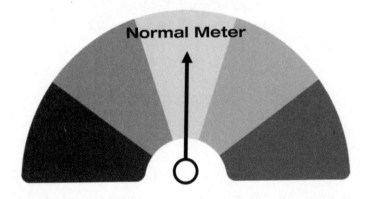

this chapter, Stage Five often falls short on delivering the happiness and fulfillment that you want or expect or will last. These things, along with your best life motivated by passion and purpose, await you in the next two stages.

Stage Five is the most emotionally neutral or dispassionate of all the stages. When making a life change—bringing something new into their lives or taking something out of it—Fives are the most likely to objectively evaluate how it fits in with everything else and affects the big picture of their lives. For example, when deciding whether or not to buy a new house, it is your Stage Five self that runs the numbers to determine whether the purchase is financially wise or investigates whether the house is in the right neighborhood and has access to quality schools. At Stage Five, how you feel about the house itself is incidental. Other stages, by contrast, tend to be governed more by desire or emotions—be they positive or negative.

Five is the stage that provides us with the best attitude for taking care of logistics. Chores that you do not enjoy but that still need to be done are best performed from a Stage Five frame of mind. For instance, when commuting to work, you are probably operating out of Stage Five as a means to a necessary end. Stage Five is the best attitude for managing your finances, doing your income tax, cleaning your house, taking out the trash, or backing up your computer: most people do such things merely because they need to be done. Stage Five is also the best outlook for walking your dog on a cold, rainy night when you'd rather be inside sleeping.

At Stage Five, you are not doing these chores out of a Stage Three fear or adherence to rules, but more as part of a larger choice you have made, such as maintaining your assets, having a clean house, or keeping and enjoying a dog you love. You might say we need a Stage Five frame of mind as our built-in "adult supervision" in order to get us through the day.

To the extent you are operating at Stage Five, you can now have mature relationships. You are finally capable of deep connection without being preoccupied with how

Stage Five

Stage Five is the normal or typical stage for an adult in our society. At Stage Five, you often think of yourself as a role juggler, or as the sum of all your life roles.

+ View of life at Stage Five is generally comfortable, dispassionate, or neutral.

+ Ideal attitudes and frame of mind to function best while doing what's merely necessary to keep your life together and functioning.

+ A Stage Five frame of mind is important to have at times with respect to certain relationships and activities.

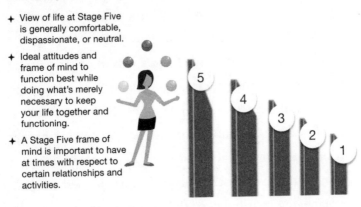

much love and approval come in your direction, as in Stage Four. For this reason, you're able to reveal much more of your true nature to those close to you without constantly fearing their judgment or rejection. This includes your spouse or significant other, family and close friends, colleagues, or anyone else important to you. True intimacy can now develop and thrive because you no longer expect others around you to be clones of yourself or serve merely as "approval machines."

At Stage Five, the role in your life that a relationship plays—including the void or slot it fills—can be incredibly important. The role might be even more significant than the people who fill it. If you are seeking a new love relationship, you might make it a mission to go out and meet suitable candidates in order to fill your relationship slot. In these cases, you would most likely become involved with the person you met that you liked the best. This is in contrast to the higher stages, where you would be unlikely even to think about a permanent relationship unless there was a genuine connection to a specific person.

At this stage, you are now comfortable in your own skin. You're in a position to feel secure in a richer and deeper sense, with feelings of contentment, satisfaction, self-acceptance, and a recognition of your strengths and weaknesses. The idea of taking risks is much less intimidating than it ever could have been in Stage Four or below. You have taken certain risks. Some have not turned out so well, but you realize that you survived and have been able to use your failures as sources of insight as opposed to hindsight-based excuses for berating yourself. For this reason, you now see wisdom and value in leaving your comfort zone at times in order to expand your life and pursue your dreams. But at Stage Five, you're also likely to think of yourself as the sum total of your roles.

A Stage Five marriage or love relationship is about filling various roles as well: lover, friend, coparent, financial partner, tennis partner, confidant, roommate, travel companion, someone to share intimacy with. But the relationship is not necessarily fueled by passion or a strong attachment that transcends the partners' roles, which is what most couples aspire to, at least when starting a long-term relationship. Those virtues become a requirement in Stage Six.

Alicia and Paul: "Our marriage worked really well until our youngest went off to college. We'd always thought that when we became empty-nesters, life for us would be easier. But instead we started having problems we'd never had before, until we realized that not having children around left a tremendous void in our marriage. What worked for us was to start a part-time business we run together. It's become another 'child.'" For Alicia and Paul, this Stage Five solution—replacing one role with another—was the answer, for now. For others, substituting grandchildren or finding a way to live vicariously through their adult children would be other examples of a Stage Five solution.

Some couples who related well at Stage Four might find themselves growing apart at Stage Five, when a partner no longer has the need for constant validation, then realizes that the relationship provides little else. The same possibility exists when one partner stops adequately fulfilling his or her role, such as sex partner, breadwinner, or coparent. In these cases, a relationship that wasn't previously at risk may stop working for both partners.

On the other hand, in many marriages that started out in the higher stages but are no longer as passionate, the partners choose to stay together and even flourish in the roles and needs they still do fulfill for each other, like best friends. This is common, as many couples are content to operate at Stage Five permanently. But for others, a marriage without the higher degrees of passion and sexual desire leads to infidelity or the realization that the relationship is no longer working.

Your career at Stage Five operates under a similar philosophy. If the ultimate Stage Four career fantasy is to become famous or acclaimed, the definitive Stage Five dream is to be rich or at least financially comfortable enough to not be beholden to anyone. Work fulfills the breadwinner role, providing external rewards such as money, acceptable hours, good working conditions, and an easy commute. This is all to enable you to afford and enjoy the lifestyle you desire. Thus the compatibility of your work with your other roles is of paramount importance. To the extent that your career is at Stage Five, you would probably choose to be spending your time in other ways if you didn't need the money or other things such as the benefits, the group affiliation, or connections that work provides. Enjoying your work at Stage Five is optional. It is not yet a part of your soul, life purpose, or calling—no matter how good at it you may be. Also at Stage Five, you don't yet require that your work make a contribution to the larger world.

Boredom or discontent with one's job or career is extremely common at this stage. When someone asks why you do your type of work, a typical Stage Five answer is likely to be, "Because that's my job," or to cite the money, pension plan, or other tangible rewards your job provides you with. If you are a writer at Stage Five, you are less likely to be doing a certain project because of anything you yourself have to say. Instead, your motives will probably be pay, recognition, or the opportunity for additional work. Schoolteachers operating at Stage Five are likely to be more motivated by summers off, benefit packages, shorter hours, and job security than by the enjoyment of teaching or the opportunity to shape the lives of students.

At Stage Five, the idea of leaving a job you don't particularly like, but which provides more money and benefits than another job you may enjoy more, might feel unthinkable—or at least could create a difficult conflict—unless that better-paying job had too many negatives or interfered with other important areas of your life or your overall sense of well-being.

Marcia: "I got laid off from my job as a bank manager as part of a major downsizing of the company. I was devastated—angry, depressed, and very scared about my future. But what surprised me the most was that I was not motivated to get another job in the banking field, where I'd worked for twenty-five years. It was the money, benefits, prestige, and security that I missed. That I was selected to be one of those let go enraged me like nothing I'd experienced before. After much soul searching, I decided to make a career change to the travel industry. Now I am actually grateful for the layoff, as it was a wake-up call that pushed me toward doing what I really wanted to do." In her career Marcia made the climb to Stage Six that she might never have considered on her own had it not been for the crisis that was triggered by losing her job. This prompted her to look at other parts of her life as well. Her story is a comparatively common one.

At Stage Five, you can take on any number of roles at the same time—leader, follower, student, mentor, or hero. Even hobbies take on a slot that you want to fill in your life, such as that of killing excess time or providing a social outlet. Exercise helps you to maintain your role as a fit and healthy person. Sporting events may fill the role of providing a family activity for Sunday afternoons, and vacations can be used to help you recharge your batteries. These are all examples of fine motives for these activities. The degree of your actual *enjoyment*, however, is not necessarily factored in at this stage. A Stage Five vacation might involve visiting a country you've never been to, then seeing and busily doing as much as time permits, even though you have no heartfelt curiosity about the place. A similar example is going to a resort you never really cared to visit because you need somewhere to go for vacation and it's a bargain.

At Stage Five, you may still at times cling to the status quo. Unplanned voids in your life can be quite troubling. You may experience the feelings of loneliness associated with going through divorce or separation or the death of a loved one. You may also feel anxious, even panicky, about the loss of a job or career, as Marcia did; a change in financial or social status; retirement; a serious illness; or the loss of membership in a group that's important to you.

Even though you may usually feel content, at times a major setback can make it seem as if your entire life is falling apart. When this happens, you might temporarily revert back to Stage Four and experience the same symptoms of anxiety, depression, or anger that are typical of conflict at that stage. During reflective moments, however, you know you've been here before and will bounce back as soon as the crisis is over or you have a strategy to handle it. At Stage Four, you may not have been able to realize this or to come back to a normal frame of mind without more difficulty. Therefore at Stage Five, even a full-blown emotional crisis is generally shorter, tends to feel less devastating, and is easier to resolve. Resolution happens as soon as the void is filled again or you realize you can cope with it.

Jim, the CEO of a highly successful company: "Once I achieved the position I'd worked for for my entire career, it became so much a part of my identity that I began to live in constant fear of somehow losing it. The job itself is by definition a stressful one, but that kind of stress I can easily handle. I managed to bring infinitely *more* stress to myself by believing that my entire well-being and that of my family's depended on my staying in this role. There was no *actual* reason to have this fear! It wasn't until I imagined losing my job and actually made a list of what I would do if this happened that I realized I had many options and we would all be OK. The stress I created in my head was far worse than any job stress I could ever experience."

Happiness And Success at Stage Five

 Keeping all roles and relationships in balance and without problems

 Being effective and not overwhelmed

 Achieving affluence

 Finding a hobby and making time for fun activities as another important way to balance life and "recharge batteries"

As Jim learned, stress is that *what-if* fear. *What if* whatever I dread (losing my status, job, or relationship; failing at something important; experiencing rejection or humiliation) did occur? We popularly call it stress, but overwhelm, anxiety, depression, and self-doubt are more appropriate labels. Recognizing, facing, and coming up with a plan for the worst thing that can happen, as Jim did (and as we discussed as a strategy in chapter 6), is a great time-tested tool for keeping this brand of Stage Five stress in check.

Success, happiness, and fulfillment at Stage Five normally result when you believe that you are handling all of your roles well, there are no major problems to deal with, and you have met your abundance goals, or at the very least are getting all you are entitled to for your efforts. Fives often speak of the good times as "feeling so normal!" Spirituality can now be more of an individual matter. For many, that opens the door for adding a spiritual element to their relationships, as well as a heartfelt awareness of the world that's greater than you are. At Stage Five, think of these things as seeds to be grown and refined in the higher stages. Unlike in the lower stages, the higher being you worship or your own higher self is much more than an authority to fear or to please. Instead it contains the messages that you *choose* to live by. You can now experience your spirituality as a solid source of connection, love, and benevolence. You may find yourself beginning to think about what your place on earth might be in spiritual terms. Too often, however, other responsibilities and aspects of life may conflict with your ability to follow that inner voice, which does not become a constant and essential part of your day-to-day life until stages Six and Seven. More likely, you will experience spirituality as merely another role that you see in a neutral way—as external—and you may have little drive within yourself for the activities or practices.

At Stage Five, your own values and those of your religion can coexist in certain areas, yet can conflict in others. You can now appreciate, as never before, the fact that growth and learning often come from a difference of opinion or even through mixed messages. Thus you now have a tolerance for those whose thinking is radically different from yours.

The principles of most organized religions are generally sources of goodness, guidance, and wisdom. Places of worship often fulfill the role of community and can provide much support when you are grieving over a death, are in crisis, or wish to celebrate a major life milestone, such as a wedding, baptism, bar mitzvah, or child's confirmation. It's common for Fives to move in and out of their spiritual community as their need for community increases or decreases. And remember—this is all within the definition of what's normal, or most commonly believed or practiced in our society. As always, you should judge what's optimal for yourself.

At this stage, you will finally be able to command respect without demanding it and can accept that others (including your significant other, children, and closest friends) will be and think differently from you. In the lower stages, there is much more difficulty with this concept.

Nonetheless, when your roles become incompatible with those around you, anxiety may still result.

In my practice, I have had many people at this stage ponder the question: "Which role (or who) is the real me?" Another question often asked as part of the struggle with Stage Five issues is one that Peggy Lee immortalized in her song "Is That All There Is?", which leads one to question such things as the meaning of life, the existence of an afterlife, and even God's role in tragedy and injustice.

Fives can be very much like plate spinners or master jugglers. Consider all of your roles in life as plates that need to be kept in the air at the same time. As long as they stay up there, life is good. In some of the roles you play, you may be kind. Other roles may require you to be rather cold. Just as you can have many roles, there is no limit to how many personae you can employ in Stage Five. One necessary skill in keeping it all together is picking the right persona or subpersonality to optimize the role you are playing. Even Captain Bligh—the tyrannical captain of *Mutiny on the Bounty* fame—is acknowledged to have been a loving husband and father, while remaining infamous as one of the cruelest ship officers of all time.

Life today, with many different roles, often means extreme busyness. Your roles might include an involved career, activities with professional organizations, hobbies and various other avocations, church or synagogue activities, and raising children, while keeping up with all your other obligations. These roles all speak to different needs, but as they grow, Fives often experience life as overwhelming to the point where enjoying any of them becomes difficult or impossible, even if each role by itself were nourishing and enjoyable. Thus, when overwhelm sets in, things on which you once thrived can become reduced to mere obligations or sources of stress, and enjoying them as you once did becomes a luxury for which you no longer have the time or energy.

Ruth and William: "We found ourselves drifting apart, but thankfully caught it in time. Our lives were just too busy! By the time the kids went to bed, we did our email,

Overwhelm

Fives can be very much like plate spinners and master jugglers.

Roles all speak to different needs.

When overwhelm sets in, things you once thrived on can inadvertently become reduced to mere obligations or even stressors.

"I wish I hadn't worked so hard."

and took care of everything else that needed to be done by the next day, we were tired and ready to go to sleep. Our sex life was on the decline, and we had no time to just relax and hang out together. We realized that we were piling too many extracurricular activities on the kids—music lessons, sports, ballet, Sunday School, and more—all in addition to their regular schoolwork. In other words, we were training them to lead a life of overwhelm like we were, and all with the best of intentions! The saddest part was that their enjoyment of their activities suffered, as did our enjoyment of ours. It's so easy to get into this pattern, and quite a challenge to turn it around, but we did and are all better off for it." I'll offer some strategies for changing this type of situation later in the chapter.

As we've done with the other stages so far, let's now look at what powers our problematic Stage Five hooks. Here are some of the attitudes and beliefs about yourself that could be creating issues for you at this stage.

- "I feel trapped, with no way out. I have no choices—my life runs me."
- "Life is full of obligations that I must personally meet and often don't enjoy."
- "I must keep it all together. I must step up to the plate with all of my roles and duties whether or not they are satisfying for me."
- "I cannot tolerate the void caused by _____ [a lost job, ended relationship, etc.]. I can't rest until I fill that slot immediately."
- "If I ask for help in fulfilling a role or obligation, it means I am weak."
- "In reality, I have it all, but still feel unfulfilled."

Which of these Stage Five themes most speak to you? If any do, take note. Then make a customized list of your own variations on them, and then commit yourself to making necessary changes in your attitudes and life. How have the ones you've identified affected your stress level, relationships, your career, and overall enjoyment of life? Once again, take note of this, along with how your life could improve if you removed the obstacles that prevent you from being fully in charge of your life. And think of this as your principal reason for managing those Stage Five hooks.

Having said that, don't lose sight of how your *non-problematic* Stage Five hooks may be serving you. You may, for example, find that preserving the status quo is your choice. Or you may choose to be involved in activities that are emotionally neutral at best (such as doing chores, dealing with certain family members, commuting, or paying the bills); to interact with people you would otherwise avoid; or to handle obligations and tasks that your job or role requires (such as doing expense reports, studying for an exam, or writing a thesis). When your choice is to be content with external rewards such as earning money and other benefits, or when comfort, security, and satisfaction are enough for you, honor that decision.

At the same time, as Ruth and William discovered, too many activities and roles can drain your quality of life. In their case, a marriage with too many obligations and activities left little or no time for them to be lovers or enjoy solitary downtime. The main thing to remember about Stage Five is to enjoy what you can, but not to expect more fulfillment than is actually there. Personal fulfillment is much more a function of stages Six and Seven.

Comfort and even affluence, a nice, decent family life, an adequate community, religious involvement, the demands you put on yourself to keep it all together, as well as all the staples of what we believe to constitute a good life, don't always add up to happiness or fulfillment. If this resonates with you, you may be yearning for something more.

That is what we will find at Stage Six, when we go beyond the boundaries of what is merely normal.

Taking Charge of Your Life: What You Need to Know to Navigate Stage Five and Move Beyond It

A bit of history is in order here. When the human-potential movement of the 1960s and 1970s took hold, the people it served the most were Fives, who, by societal standards, had a good life—a well-functioning career, family life, and relationships—but through their higher-stage hooks knew they could achieve a richer, more fulfilling inner existence. In reality, they were looking for the ladder to climb from Stage Five to the two highest stages. Encounter groups and other types of personal-growth opportunities, which were extremely innovative at the time, were created to encourage people to take the steps necessary for leaving their comfort zones.

The result was often one or more major life changes as well as a range of new and unfamiliar, yet empowering, attitudes. For example, long-term love relationships and career activities would now have to provide deeper levels of fulfillment. For many Fives, a radical makeover—a divorce, career, or lifestyle change—was in order, while for others a bit of tweaking was all that was necessary. Most interestingly, all of this was accomplished by simply and nonjudgmentally prodding each seeker to ask, "What do *I* want to do?" and "What do *I* want *my* life to be?" The next step was to establish the self-permission to go ahead and do it. In other words, individuals were to encouraged to keep the roles that were satisfying, while making whatever changes were necessary to the roles that no longer worked. Along with taking action, it was just as important to change certain attitudes and life philosophies so that people did not find themselves going backwards in the familiar direction of nonfulfillment.

The result was a new world that would never allow things to be the way they were. For example, it was now time to maximize opportunity and equality for women and minorities and to grant permission for everyone to follow their dreams and passions. In fact, we came to know that an attitude of self-permission is the essential ingredient for living your best life or reaching your highest potential.

Here are some examples of those attitudes and beliefs that, when hardwired, will give you self-permission to access this zone of passion and purpose, which is the essential ingredient for living your life in the two highest stages—those of your highest potential:

- "I want to be doing what I love and to feel rewarded *internally* as well as externally." (This is perhaps the most important attitude for making the climb to Stage Six.)
- "I can handle being overwhelmed."

- "I resolve to use those times when I feel overwhelmed as learning experiences that can help me decide what to keep in my life or whether to take on something new."
- "Satisfaction and gratification are nice to have, but I accept that there are many things I choose to have in my life that don't provide them to the extent that I wish they would." (This is an important attitude to have toward things in your life that cry out for a Stage Five frame of mind.)
- "I can ask for help from others without getting down on myself."
- "I have the power to change my life."
- "Not everything is meant to be a source of joy and fulfillment."

1. Just as you did those with the affirmations in the previous stages, pick the ones from the list above that speak to you the most. Then write them on a three-by-five card or put them into your smartphone for easy access.

2. The Buddha said it best in the quote with which I opened this chapter, which is arguably the most powerful statement ever made about how to reach your potential: "Be open to everything but attached to nothing." Consider making this the core attitude that will most empower you from now on.

Moving from Stage Five to Stage Six simply involves letting go of the roles that are not working or are obsolete—that you keep solely because of your attachment to them—and then trading them for new experiences that ignite or feed your unique gifts and passions.

3. If necessary, find a mentor, coach, or therapist to support you in making the changes you find difficult to make on your own. Perhaps some new role models are in order. At Stage Five and beyond, having heroes who have already achieved goals for which you are now striving can provide both inspiration and direction. The best mentors are usually those who are more advanced or successful in your field, or who are further along with your most difficult challenges. Just be sure that whomever you work with has walked the walk and is comfortable with helping you to explore and facilitate your own chosen life changes. This is perhaps even more important at this stage and beyond than it is in any of the lower stages.

Some people leave one marriage or love relationship—whether or not by their own choice—only to enter into a new one immediately and on the rebound. The same holds true when you quickly replace a lost job with another, similar one without even asking whether a bigger life change may be in order. This "solution" of replacing one role, job, or love relationship with another one is a very common way that Fives stay stuck. It's also the principal reason that rebound romances rarely deliver long-term fulfillment.

Part of the climb to Stage Six is accepting and tolerating some emotional pain when there's a void in your life until you can replace the missing piece with what you really desire. That way you will break your pattern of settling for whatever is available to you right now—be it a new relationship, job, or anything else—simply in order to end the discomfort. Most importantly, you will have given yourself much more than just another Band-Aid to get you through a difficult transition.

4. Try this simple drop-out exercise, which was quite helpful to Ruth and William. It's also one of my personal favorites: *Imagine yourself completely dropping all of your roles, obligations and current relationships. Pretend for a moment that there are absolutely no sacred cows in your life and that you can be free of anything and everything that consumes your time and energy.* As you make this imaginary housecleaning as thoroughly as possible, make a list of everything you are leaving behind, which constitutes your life as it now is. When your list is complete, it will be a summary of your present life. *Once again, imagine your life without all of the roles, people, obligations and other things on your list. Then take a moment to savior this feeling of absolute freedom.* (Some people experience

this as a George Bailey moment, as in the movie *It's a Wonderful Life*.)

When you have that image and are ready to move on, it's time to start your next list. Only in this one, include first whom and what (roles and things) you really want to put back into your life. Make sure that it's your desires that are speaking to you, not what you think *should* be included in your new list.

When this second list is complete, make one final list. This one will include whatever is in your second list (what you would like to put back into your life), but which cries out for change—major or minor—before you choose to include it unconditionally. The purpose of this third list is to recognize what relationships need some work; what roles you want to be more or less involved with and under what circumstances; and anything else in your life that you want or need to keep, but which need some degree of fine-tuning. As you do this, you may come to recognize many shades of gray, as well as what is more black-and-white!

For each item you want to change, ask yourself, "If I were not attached to a role (such as breadwinner, husband or wife, father or mother, son or daughter, boss, subordinate, fund-raising chairman, friend, or neighbor), what would be the ideal situation for this aspect of my life?" How do you believe this part of your life could be simpler, more enjoyable, more purposeful, and less overwhelming? Never forget that Stage Five can also be your chosen stage for such aspects of life as your marriage or career. *If that is your choice, honor it!* Consider this exercise to be a thorough mental housecleaning. Personally, I do this often.

5. Many Stage Five issues, such as feeling overwhelmed, can be addressed by learning time-management skills and becoming comfortable with saying no to requests that will pile more onto you without giving much back. Juggling a busy schedule, multiple roles, and things such as children's activities and work obligations is daunting. But don't fall into the trap of believing that there are no options. Instead, take this opportunity to clarify what's truly important to you.

In addition, keep in mind that sometimes trading one role for another, similar one is indeed the best solution to a crisis or dilemma. Thus keeping Stage Five solutions in your arsenal is also important. Whatever may be your chosen approach, you will serve yourself well by regularly clarifying what you wish to keep in your life and what you wish to discard or modify, and then by taking whatever appropriate action these insights prompt you to choose.

Resolve to do as little as necessary of whatever you have chosen to discontinue. Expect some discomfort.

Whenever you give up a role, the void that is created can bring about some uneasiness. Don't get discouraged. Assure yourself there is something far better for you ahead, even if you don't see exactly what that may be at this moment. For starters, you can resolve to enjoy the gift of the extra time you've gotten. Act as if the void is only a temporary one, soon to be replaced by what you truly desire—unless you've decided that you don't need this role in any form.

Remember, Stage Five is the most neutral or dispassionate stage. Stage Five chores and activities are often the necessary means for maximizing life at the highest stages. If you don't expect more satisfaction from doing them than is actually there, you will be less likely to fight them, procrastinate, or waste more time. And *your expectations are the one thing that is always under your control!*

To get to Stage Five, your task was to reduce dependency, depression, anxiety, stress, and anger, and to increase self-discipline, self-confidence, courage, and your tolerance for frustration. All of this made it possible to function in your chosen roles. The climb to Stage Six makes all this hard work profoundly worthwhile, as we rise above our roles and enter the zone where we are finally, firmly, and internally guided by our own passions and values!

Entering the Zone of Your Highest Potential

What else do you need to look at, change or take care of before we enter that zone of your highest potential?

Entering the Zone of Your Highest Potential—Your Best Life

Now that you have read about the first five stages, and perhaps have applied some of the strategies to your life, it's time to reap the rewards!

The task now is to take the next (and most exciting and enjoyable) step in your Stage Climbing process. When you're operating out of stages Six and Seven, you're using the most *unique, evolved, purposeful,* and perhaps the *best* parts of yourself to achieve. On a spiritual level, you're attuned to your calling or purpose and to the wisdom that defines it. On a personal level, this is where you love others, are most creative and—just in case that's not enough—feel best about yourself. Stages Six and Seven characterize the life you were *born* to live!

So let's start thinking about what your highest potential looks like. Or to phrase it another way, as many people I've worked with have, "What do you *really* want to be when you grow up?"

This can be life-changing. The next two chapters will show you exactly how to make operating from this zone of your highest potential second nature.

Target Stages: Your Life's Purpose

Stages Six and Seven are the stages that most people aspire to—your "target stages."

This is your best life!

It's your passion and purpose-driven life where fulfillment and happiness is *internally* generated.

It's the *zone of your highest potential—the life you were born to live—where* you are using *the best parts of yourself* to accomplish almost anything!

CHAPTER EIGHT

Stage Six
Follow Your Passion

*I have learned that if one advances confidently in the direction
of his dreams and endeavors to live the life which he has
imagined, he will meet with an unexpected success.*
—HENRY DAVID THOREAU

What do you most enjoy? What makes you so motivated
that you need only your own satisfaction to do it, and nobody else even has to notice? What or whom do you truly
love? What excites you so much that it keeps begging for
your attention, even if you try to ignore it? What *inspires*
you, or most puts you *in spirit*? What makes you feel *best*
about yourself? Let me suggest that you keep these questions in mind as you read about Stage Six.

Now let's assume that all of your problematic lower-stage
hooks are either out of the picture entirely or under your
control. You've let go of past pain and victimhood, as well as
all of the anxieties that were holding you back. What now?

Alan: "I have everything going for me—a successful business, a loving family, and an enviable lifestyle. But I don't feel happy or fulfilled. In other words, I *should* be happy, but I am not, and don't know why. My doctor thought I was depressed and prescribed me an antidepressant, but it didn't really help."

Alan didn't realize it when he first came to me, but on his own he had masterfully navigated the first five stages. It immediately became apparent that Alan's depression and unhappiness were nature's way of telling him he'd hit an impasse. He "had it all"—that is, everything but a mission that he could passionately pursue. When he was building his business, that need was fulfilled. He felt challenged then. But now that the business was hugely successful, his sense of purpose was gone. Furthermore, nobody around him could understand his dilemma: "Life is good, so what's the problem?" We'll revisit Alan later.

For most people, Stage Six is the very definition of a genuine connection to your purpose, creativity, happiness, and fulfillment. Life characteristically feels at its best when we are operating out of this stage. As you read on, you will clearly see how this first stage in that zone of your highest potential resides within you. It is waiting for you to access it right now and apply it to any part of your life.

Think about our evolution as human beings. For much of our existence, we worked to survive and married mainly to procreate and share our chores. When there was

Stage Six is the very definition of a genuine connection to your purpose, creativity, happiness, and fulfillment.

Life characteristically feels at its absolute best when we're operating out of this stage.

But the fact is that...

The quest for enjoyment and fulfillment as we know it today is relatively new in our evolution!

free time, we would likely sleep or do things related to survival. Today, instead of spending time hand-washing clothes, we are free to read a book or watch a football game while a machine does it for us. The quest for enjoyment and fulfillment as we know it today is relatively new in our history, but it would be an understatement merely to say that this concept has caught on. Ideally, today we marry for love and strive to do the type of work that's most personally gratifying. An entire book could be written (and many have been) simply about things we do and industries that have been devised to gratify us or help us to feel happy. This is all possible because we now have the time, skills, technology, and resources to give attention to those parts of ourselves that seek higher levels of gratification. For most people who live in developed countries, fulfillment has now become even more of an issue than survival!

Your frame of mind at Stage Six can be described as simply the fulfillment that comes to you as a result of living the life you were born to live. And it is our unique passions that lead us to this zone within ourselves.

Life at your highest potential is a wonderful occasion. Fully rising to that occasion means becoming something far greater than your roles. This is the breakthrough to Stage Six. This stage can also be seen as a new definition of positive mental health. Whether you're already there or not, you'll probably agree that Stage Six is worth aspiring toward for just about any part of your life.

The Buddha often used the sun's constant presence in the sky as a metaphor for the natural order of things. Even if clouds and storms block the sun's light, you know it's still there. Think of the sun as a metaphor for your passions. Then imagine your fears and your problematic lower-stage hooks as the clouds and storms that are blocking this sun from shining through. This inner turbulence is what blocks your natural Stage Climbing process. To the extent that you are living in Stage Six, you've managed to navigate or see through those storms and clouds. If you recognize obstacles that are still blocking you in some way, including old hurts you have not let go of and people against whom you still carry resentment, make note of them. Resolve to use every tool at your disposal, in this book as well as all

Stage Six
First of Two Target Steps

Stage Six is a "mature" adult—as determined by your not by your chronological age, but by the way you conduct your life—with a strong integrity and sense of self.

+ Rise above your roles.

+ Operate according to your own unique and internally generated values and passions.

+ These become your driving forces.

+ Genuine fulfillment, spirituality, and happiness result.

+ You love, enjoy, excel, and create in your own distinct way.

the other resources available to you, to work toward permanently eliminating these obstacles.

In Stage Five, your roles define you. At Stage Six, all of that changes. Furthermore, you are no longer ruled by your ego. Instead your inner voice now takes command and guides you. The roles you play now revolve around you instead of controlling or defining you. Your unique talents and passions—along with the self-permission to pursue them to the fullest—are what launch you to Stage Six. Instead of shifting your personality to meet the demands of each role you play (although you can still do that when you choose), you are now in touch with a strong, consistent, and solid layer of integrity within you that holds them all together. This is your core, or at least the seed of it. Just like the sun, it's been there all along; but at

Stage Six you're finally allowing it to shine through and take center stage.

At Stage Six, your passions and the internal rewards they give you are now more meaningful to you than anything you could receive from outside of yourself. Up until now, in stages One through Five, your main sources of motivation—financial status, recognition, praise, approval, even survival—principally depended on forces outside of your own skin and often out of your control. Listening to your passions and living your life was a bonus—actually a Stage Six hook—but was not yet your highest priority.

Hooks at Stage Six actually begin to appear in childhood. You're operating out of Stage Six whenever you're doing what you are best at, when you're motivated by your desires and pursuing what you truly enjoy. That includes loving others in your life or doing labors of love for them; being uniquely creative; and acting in accordance with your purpose and calling.

As a Six, you can understand and interact with those in the lower stages without feeling threatened, being preoccupied with fitting in, needing to be like anyone else, or needing anyone else to be like you. You understand and value the virtues of uniqueness, so you no longer need to live vicariously through anyone, including your children. You have your own life and honor the right of those around you to live theirs. You are much more able to conduct your life without inner conflict.

Passion

*What you love and what you hate (or dislike intensely)
are your passions at their most extreme.*

Negative passions tell us what we need to avoid or get away from, such as a bad marriage, an unfulfilling career, or toxic people.

Our positive passions are the engine or life force behind our creativity, our ability to love others deeply, to enjoy, and to accomplish great things.

**Ignoring your passions can rob you of a huge slice
of what life at its best has to offer you.**

At this stage, you become a peer to your mentors. (Sometime mentors even have unexpected or negative reactions to how you have evolved, by virtue of their own lower-stage hooks.) Chances are you have pushed the envelope, and you have discovered that it is no longer frightening to leave your comfort zone, and it can even feel exhilarating. So taking prudent risks has become a nonissue, rather than a trigger for anxiety or an excuse for avoidance.

What you love and what you hate (or dislike intensely) are your passions at their most extreme. (Thus a passion can be a feeling of strong, positive, gut-level excitement on the one hand, or of intense negativity on the other.) Ignoring your passions can rob you of a huge slice of what life has to offer you. The opposite approach is to listen to them so that they become your reliable inner guides. Our positive passions—the things we love, the things that put us most in touch with feelings of joy and our life's purpose—are the engine behind our creativity and our ability to love others, to enjoy, and to accomplish great things.

Passion is the best currency to help you accomplish what you want. The stronger your passion for something, the more you will become committed to it. Most of the world's truly accomplished people would probably agree that passion and the willingness to be guided by it are among the most important ingredients of their success. That's why passion is your path to the zone of your highest potential.

Few things are as rewarding as connecting with the positive passion within you, knowing how to call upon it at any time, how to utilize it maximally, and how to give yourself permission to access this zone at will. This includes choosing to be childlike, to play and experience fun, joy, and happiness, as you may have at earlier times in your life. At Stage Six, your adult self has no problem letting your inner child take over for a while and enjoying every minute of it to the fullest!

Negative passions are equally important, because they serve several purposes. They tell us what we need to avoid or get away from, such as a bad marriage, an unfulfilling career, or toxic people. Negative passions can also be the driving force behind a huge positive cause. Nelson Mandela and his mission to defeat apartheid is a good example.

But negative passions can also be signals of our dark side, and our most problematic lower-stage hooks usually power such things as toxic addictions. Only you can recognize the difference. That's another reason why it's crucial to understand the lower stages and to manage your hooks there by choosing how they fit into your life.

There's a condition sometimes referred to as an existential crisis, which is the result of either being out touch with or habitually ignoring your passions. This is akin to having chronic fatigue of the psyche. It can take its toll with a low-grade depression known as dysthymia, with chronic anger and bitterness, or even with a variety of serious physical conditions. Ignoring your passions amounts to joining the fight to defeat the best parts of yourself. This was the cause of Alan's depression. And this is one condition that virtually anyone can joyously overcome.

At Stage Six, doing what you love most—and doing it to your maximum satisfaction—is now an essential component of your overall happiness and well-being. You may even wish to challenge yourself to be the best there is at whatever you do—or at least to see yourself working toward that standard. To win at Stage Six is simply to enjoy what you have, whom you are close to, how you spend your time, and what you are doing. Life becomes easier and more flowing. To love, create, and enjoy is what puts you *in joy,* and that is the state of mind you are after.

Here are a few other staples of happiness and success at Stage Six that come up with consistency:

- The satisfaction of reaching a difficult goal or solving a tough problem.
- The feelings of excitement and empowerment that come from peak performance.
- Feelings of relaxation and inner peace.
- The bliss associated with the little things in everyday life, such as the glow of a nice spring day, writing poetry, reading a good book, or listening to your favorite music.
- The joy of exploring novelty and whatever stimulates you or makes you curious.
- Doing what you really want to be doing so that the distinction between work and play disappears.
- Being with and doing for those you love and feel deeply connected to.
- Letting go and calling up the child in you at will.
- Following your passions and thereby fulfilling your purpose.
- Being in the now and living in the present.

A job or career that you might have worked hard to obtain at Stage Five may be painfully unfulfilling to you at Stage Six if it merely provides financial or other external rewards. Your work is now a part of your purpose or call-

It's All Circular!

Your purpose is what most inspires you...

And your spirit is the source of your purpose...

What "inspires" puts you *in spirit*

No two of us are exactly the same when we look inwardly at our passions, desires, and talents.

ing. When you are driven by your genuine passions and desires, chances are you would choose to do the type of work you are doing even if you had enough money never to have to work again. The process of doing something you're passionate about, regardless of the outcome, is what makes it worth doing. This is partially because Stage Six activities have a reliable way of bringing out the best feelings in you. For example, if playing golf is your passion, at Stage Six the feelings of enjoyment, well-being, and self-satisfaction when playing the game will be at least as important to you as the outcome.

So our passions are a major part of what determines our purpose and calling. If you made a list of all the things you feel passionately about and are truly committed to— regardless of what anyone else may think of them—you would have a list of what constitutes the meaning of your life in the simplest possible terms. For Alan, making this list was pivotal for him in locating the missing piece in his life. Why not make that list for yourself now? Keep it handy, and add to it each time a new item occurs to you. Then consult it often as an important reminder of what your life is about.

My routine advice about picking a career has always been to do what you love and what is enjoyable and satisfying for you. This may sound obvious, but in my experience, far too few do it. In fact I have seen credible surveys over the years that found that more than four out of five people are unhappy with their careers in some way: one shocking Gallup survey from 2014 had the figure at 87 percent. You will spend a lot of time at work. In addition to the obvious benefits of enjoying it, you may use it as a standard to set for yourself in all of the other aspects of your life that are important to you.

This topic is a very personal one for me. More than anything else, it explains my decades-long mission to help people connect with and live by their passions. I started my early career as an accountant. Within a few years, while I was still in my early twenties, I started my own accounting firm, which quickly became successful and lucrative. Around the same time, I married, became a father, and seemed to have it all. But by my mid-twenties, I had become very bored with my career. It no longer had passion or challenge in it for me. Our marriage wasn't working either. After much contemplation, one by one I began making major changes in all areas of my life. Over a period of several years, I sold the firm, got divorced, went to graduate school, got a master's degree and doctorate, and then changed my career to psychology—the field I loved as a hobby, but up to then had never even thought of as a career.

When I became a psychologist, the professional climate was for me the exact opposite of that of accounting, and the rewards were incalculable! For example, it's impossible for me to not be challenged and fascinated by the complexity of each individual I work with, as well as by the vast body of knowledge that I can both learn from and contribute to. This for me was the definition of a labor of love, powered by passion and rewards that spoke to me at a very deep level. What's yours? Take a moment to reflect on that question.

I was sitting on a train recently and overheard two men talking about someone who had worked for their organization. They discussed the fact that he gave up a $250,000-a-year job for one that paid less than $50,000. They could not understand why, and thought he had lost his mind. This is indeed hard to understand from the perspective of the lower stages (in this case, Stage Five). When I started, following my passion for psychology was certainly not a wise financial decision either, but I discovered what so many others have found: when you are doing what you were born to do, the money eventually finds you as well.

In my practice, I've helped many people in virtually every field and profession to make career changes as they got out of lucrative fields such as medicine, law, and successful family businesses. The reason: they could not happily continue doing the work they were doing because of their missing sense of purpose and lack of passion. As previously noted, that was certainly a reason I switched from accounting (Stages Three and Five) to psychology (solidly Stage Six) early in my career. Yet many of my old accounting colleagues still do that kind of work and love it. For them, accounting represents a wonderful Stage Six career choice, whereas for me it simply could not. In Alan's case, depression was his wake-up call. In mine, it was simply the chronic and painful dissatisfaction of not feeling challenged.

Kenneth, a forty-year-old former corporate attorney who changed his specialty to prosecuting criminals: "Had you asked me why I worked in corporate back then, I would have pointed to the money and perks or said, 'I'd go nuts if I weren't doing *something*.' I was earning over eight times as much as I make now as a prosecutor. But now that I love what I do and am very good at it, the answer is a lot easier. Even though I am making much less money, I wouldn't want to be doing anything else. My work has a purpose, and I look forward to stepping up to the plate and meeting the many challenges of it every day. No amount of money could ever replace that. If I ever make another career change, it would have to be from a combination of hearing another calling and no longer feeling as passionate about my present work." Kenneth went on to say that if he were wealthy enough never to have to work again or there were no money to pay him, he'd do exactly what he's doing without pay. His attitude is typical of many who have climbed from Stage Five to Stage Six in their careers.

I believe that there's a vocation in each of us that can trigger this kind of Stage Six response. Of course, earning a lot of money for doing something you love enough to do for free is what most people would consider a grand slam. Moreover, I routinely argue, from both personal and professional experience, that when you are doing what you truly enjoy and were born to do, you are one of the richest people on the planet!

But if you haven't yet found what that something is for you, regardless of your circumstances—age, obligations, or any other reasons you believe stand in your way—use every resource available to intensify that search until you do discover it. And anyone committed to this path can! Many of the strategies in this chapter will help you get there.

Sixes can be quite vulnerable to job and career burnout. This is most common in two situations: when workplace frustrations conflict with your attempts to accomplish a task or a creative mission; and when your passion changes or evolves to another level that your present job or career simply cannot satisfy. The term *burnout* wisely uses the metaphor of fire. In my experience, those who are most likely to burn out are the very people who are or were most "on fire" in their commitment to what they do.

For example, at one point in my career I oversaw all of the psychological services of the Philadelphia police department. I noticed that burnout occurred frequently with the officers who were most dedicated to their jobs—those who were considered the best of the best (Stage Six) and who looked upon their work as their mission or calling. On the other hand, burnout was almost nonexistent among Stage Five (and lower) officers, who sought easy assignments and who freely admitted that they were there merely for the job security, pension, early retirement (some could actually tell you the number of days to their retirement a decade or more beforehand), and other tangible rewards of being a police officer.

Here are some typical Stage Six attitudes about your career and the work you do:

- "I love what I do and feel at my best about myself when I am doing it."
- "It's what comes easiest to me. It feels most flowing and natural."
- "I feel fulfilled irrespective of the financial and other external rewards I get."
- "I get off on the challenge of it."
- "If I were the wealthiest person on earth, I would still choose to be doing this."

The affirmation that delivers these feelings is simply this: *listen to the message your passions send you, and the best course of action will be apparent.*

When you are acting according to your purpose, you are inspired or *in spirit*, and it is actually that inspiration which blurs the lines between work and fun. At Stage Six, you are now likely to spend as little time as possible with anything—work, hobbies, or people—that does not inspire you on some level.

As you become more and more inwardly motivated, you become less and less dependent on anything out of your reach. In part, the human species is the most evolved because of a characteristic that we take for granted but which makes us distinctive: no two of us want exactly the same things when we look inwardly at our passions, desires, and talents. And that source of fulfillment is available to you twenty-four hours a day, seven days a week. You only have to remember to seek and connect with it. Some of the most consistently successful people are those who can line up their passions, talents, intentions, obsessions, and ambitions—then let them reinforce each other in order to create their own distinctive brand of magic. After that, wealth and abundance are on track to follow almost as an effortless by-product.

Passion is also a crucial factor in your love relationships, parenting, hobbies, community involvement, and virtually everything else that's important to you. Your interests in theater, opera, travel, politics, reading, learning, sports, writing, and of course sex are parts of your life driven to some degree by passion. If you tend to be politically liberal or conservative at Stage Six, you're operating out of an inner commitment to the principles and values that match your core beliefs. As you've probably noticed, this is quite the opposite of such things as guilt, envy, fear, and rigidity, or the need to fit in with or impress others who have similar beliefs.

Over the years, many people have told me that they have never been passionate about anything. But I can't think of anyone who could not find passion in themselves regarding something. If you are an avid baseball fan or basketball player; movie or theater buff; dancer or swimmer; gourmet cook; or really enjoy sex, a good novel, a concert, or poetry, then you have the capacity to be passionate. Yet simply having passion is not enough. It's allowing yourself to value, listen to, and act on it that transports you to the zone where you are living your best life.

When your passions are your road map, the end point may not be apparent at times. But by following them, you'll rarely be disappointed. Sometimes you might have a "been there, done that" experience. When this happens, you'll know that it's time to move on to another passion. However, being open to wherever it will take you is usually all you will need to do to ultimately get back on to the path you're seeking.

So ask yourself these questions right now: Does your career or job bring you happiness and fulfillment? Is there anything else you'd rather be doing? How about your marriage or love relationship or lack thereof? Is this part of your life working as you want it to? Are other major aspects of your life bringing you the sense of purpose, happiness, and fulfillment you seek from them? What are you willing to work on to achieve this feeling? What in your life warrants a deeper commitment? What needs to be eliminated? Perhaps most importantly, what areas of your life trigger in you the best feelings about yourself? I suggest you write out your reflections regarding these questions as well as others that come to mind, and make the exploration of them an ongoing exercise.

There are two things that I have lightheartedly referred to as "passion disorders." One is obviously when passion is missing. The other is when passion is so important that there is a tendency to neglect anything you are *not* passionate about. For example, you may have little or no passion for your job or the work you do, even though it's necessary to show up in order to make a living (Stage Five). Then you may allow your passion for playing computer games and surfing the Internet to take priority over your job responsibilities, perhaps causing you career and financial problems. At Stage Six, you're able to accept reality even when you don't like it. You can do what makes the most *long-term* sense without conflict. You may, for example, mind your job responsibilities and temporarily put aside the things you enjoy more while developing a long-term strategy for a job change that allows you to do what you really want to be doing.

The journey to your passionate self is often a lonely one, because nobody else can tell you what you are or should or should not be passionate about. Moreover, neither you nor I consciously choose our passions! In fact, passions actually choose or call upon you. This is why we commonly refer to a passion or purpose as a *calling*. Once you hear a passion calling, you have the choice of whether or not to acknowledge it and act on it. This principle certainly applies to career preferences, people you're attracted to, and even the foods you enjoy. You can choose your behavior (such as whether to eat that piece of cheesecake), and the people you associate with or make love to, but not your desires themselves. This chapter gives you the questions to ask yourself, along with strategies to help you access those passionate parts of yourself that constitute your Stage Six core.

Spirituality for Sixes is a highly individual matter, and no definition of spirituality at this stage is complete without using the terms *unique* and *higher self*. Your higher self is the internal part of you that is connected to your unique image of God, a Godlike higher power within you, or a cosmic and energetic connection that can be expressed in or outside of an organized religion. I personally believe in the Hindu notion that there are many possible and valid paths to God and your spiritual truth.

At Stage Six, religion may or may not be an important part of your life. Religious practices may help, but they're not necessary for you to connect to your spiritual source, because your connection to the divine can be direct. There's no longer a blur between what is religious (practices you have learned) and what is spiritual (or generated internally). It's even possible to be an atheist or an agnostic, provided that you are open to the range of other spiritual possibilities as your inner resources guide you. What's crucial for this area is that your core beliefs and convictions find you, fit you, and provide you with the inner guidance you seek.

Through practices such as meditation, yoga, journaling, journeying, visualization, or your own combination of any or all of these, you can deepen and enhance your connection to the infinite pool of resources within you. This will enable you to establish a set of spiritual beliefs and practices that are truly your own. You are likely to discover that your higher self is what connects you with your unique strengths, calling, and principles, as well as with your commitment to pursue them. Many find a spiritual connection in their important relationships or in love and awe for the beauty of nature and the world.

The more you connect to the deepest levels of this source of infinite wisdom, the more you'll discover that your spirituality, along with all of the answers you'll ever

The Stage Six Barometer

Following your passions at Stage Six...

Brings out the best feelings in you about yourself.

need to live your life optimally, exist not outside but within you, and are constantly evolving. Your challenge is to connect to this source. Any route you take to do this is a step in the right direction.

At Stage Six, you can love those you love very deeply. Loving someone else strongly resonates with you at Stage Six, and it's never grounded in fear or neediness. At Stage Four, the love that comes your way is the prime motivator. But at Stage Six, you now know that it's more gratifying to love than to be loved. Whom you love is truly a matter of your choice. But remember, you have no real power at all over who loves you. A Six saying "I love you" does not need the other person to repeat it back in order for that statement to stand. This ability to love without needing a guarantee of reciprocity can be profoundly life-changing.

Feeling good about yourself when in the presence of someone you love is a reliable indicator that for you, your relationship is at Stage Six. Working with couples in therapy, I've learned over the years that how partners say they feel about each other is not as telling as how they feel about themselves when they are with (or even thinking about) their partner.

Use this as a litmus test. It's a wonderful standard to apply to anyone who's important to you. It's also useful for determining if you are operating from Stage Six in a part of your life. Whether you are thinking about your significant other, your career or avocation, friends or groups to which you belong, the question is, *how do you feel about yourself* with respect to them? The better you feel, the more that part of your life is operating in Stage Six. For many, this alone could be enough to explain the feelings of fulfillment that make Stage Six so worthwhile.

At Stage Six, you can also be quite happy for other people, even though their good fortune does not benefit you or may even have an adverse effect upon you. For example, a Stage Six politician who lost an election could, on a personal level, be genuinely happy for his opponent's good fortune (and not just for the TV cameras, which would be more indicative of Stage Four), while still being appropriately sad for himself for having been defeated. An actor who lost an Oscar can be sincerely happy for the winner whom she believes also gave an excellent performance. Part of being a Six is letting go of outcomes over which we have no control.

In addition, at this stage you are now better able to disagree with someone, even on a major issue, without anger or defensiveness, and without thinking less of that individual merely because you disagree. You are also above envy. Although you can be extraordinarily competitive, you know your life, mission, and circumstances are distinctly your own and could never be accurately compared to anyone else's.

At Stage Six, you will be unlikely to stay in a marriage or love relationship that's dysfunctional or unfulfilling. Remember that it's now the *person* that you're connected to, not the idea or role of a partner, the security or the validation he or she provides. These things no longer appeal to you enough to serve as the basis for a relationship. You've set a much higher standard for yourself. So if you find your marriage or relationship going in a bad direction, you'll either take massive action to remedy the situation or accept this painful reality and get out of it quickly. Insecurities about being alone, which may have tempted you to settle for an unfulfilling situation in the past, are no longer a factor at Stage Six.

It's interesting to note that many, if not most, love relationships begin by virtue of Stage Six hooks, with that delicious initial passion fueled by a dopamine high. Sex is often effortlessly passionate and ecstatic for each partner. Most relationships, however, experience a decrease in this

Love

The act of *loving* someone else—as opposed to being loved—is central to you at Stage Six.

A *Six* saying "I love you" does not need the other person to repeat it back.

Feeling especially good *about yourself* with respect to someone or something is a good indicator that for you your relationship is at Stage Six.

initial passion as a short-term relationship morphs into one that's long-term. But at Stage Six, your connection with your partner makes this much less of an issue.

If you are seeking a love relationship, a Stage Six frame of mind could be your greatest asset. Since I wrote my first book, *The Art of Living Single* (1989), many people have asked me what the best way is to attract a potential mate. My answer is simple: It's not about places you go or things you do. It's about your attitude toward yourself. When you are feeling good about yourself and doing what you enjoy, the energy you put out is likely to act as a magnet for attracting exactly what you want. In other words, you look more attractive, and you transmit an invitation to the type of people you are looking to attract.

While exploring romantic challenges at Stage Four, we met Dorothy, who was unable to have a long-term relationship. She was addicted to that dopamine high of new romances and overly focused on how much love was coming in her direction. By working through some of her problematic Stage Four hooks, she is now in a long-term relationship that both she and her partner see as permanent.

Dorothy: "This now sounds so obvious, but like in the title of that old song, I was 'in love with love,' not with the other person for who he was. My old short-term relationships were never with men that I would even think of as friends. This pattern might have continued indefinitely had I not decided to look at this by taking a yearlong moratorium on romantic relationships. After an exceptionally painful break-up, I made the decision not to jump into a new one. This was very difficult for me. One thing I have never had a problem doing is meeting men and becoming involved very quickly. So I took away all the pressures I'd always put on myself. I recommend this highly for anyone who is on this kind of romantic treadmill. Instead, I paid more attention to my friendships with both my male and female friends. After about a year, a romance slowly started developing between me and a male friend that I had known for many years, but had never thought of in that way. *I learned that attraction can develop!* (I'd always thought that if it wasn't there immediately, it didn't exist.) What's more, I have a love for him that feels far more genuine than anything I had felt in these whirlwind romances. Also, I never need to give a thought about his feelings for me. I know they're there and never have to ask. There isn't any jealousy either. I completely attribute this to my brand-new ability to see the person first. I feel like I finally grew up!" I believe this shift is one that anyone who wants a solid long-term relationship can quickly make.

For many relationships, as time and life go on and passions change or wane, the partners move backwards towards Stage Five. As I have pointed out in my previous books *The Art of Staying Together* (1993) and *Can Your Relationship Be Saved? How to Know Whether to Stay or Go* (2002), partners who are unwilling to work together to keep their passion alive often find themselves creating emotional distance or indifference. Sometimes this prompts an affair or a breakup, while at other times it simply reduces the marriage to a nice friendship or a dutiful collaboration of roles that then remains at Stage Five. When this happens, both partners can choose to work on whatever issues need to be dealt with in order to climb back to Stage Six together.

Most relationships at Stage Six are grounded in a sense of comfort and deep caring for each other that transcends even sex. Even though most people normally associate passion with sex, at this stage it's your partner that you are passionate about, not necessarily sex or any other activity you share. In reality, sexual desire varies greatly from person to person and can be influenced by many factors, both psychological and physiological. I have also seen many couples in my practice that report having ecstatic sex even though virtually every other aspect of the relationship is in shambles, operating at lower and sometimes even the lowest stages.

The trend toward divorce in recent decades was a revolution brought on by a sudden, collective change in consciousness about marital roles. As the pendulum swings in the other direction toward a lower divorce rate, expect more of an evolution. For this, I credit and encourage a relatively new practice in which couples *custom-design* their lifestyle together. As a result, you, as a couple, are empowered to make your own choices and to understand that each partner has as much right as the other to be passionate about his or her own needs, desires, and sources of fulfillment. Marriages that operate by dependency, intimidation, rules, insecurity, and fulfilling expected roles are less likely to survive one partner's spurt of growth into Stage Six. At the same time, breakups and divorces, triggered by partners growing in opposite directions, do certainly occur at Stage Six, as in the lower stages.

Note that at Stage Six, you can be profoundly content without any love relationship at all. Like practically everything else at this stage, choice as opposed to need prevails.

Stage Six hooks can appear at almost any age. An eight-year-old who loves her parents, siblings, or a friend in the mature way an adult would is an example of an early Stage Six hook. Child prodigies in music, art, math, science, and

Stage Six Hooks Can Appear at Almost Any Age

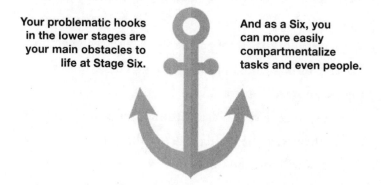

Your problematic hooks in the lower stages are your main obstacles to life at Stage Six.

And as a Six, you can more easily compartmentalize tasks and even people.

sports are other obvious examples. Most of us can recognize clues to the roots of our unique talents as far back as adolescence or early childhood. I try never to miss an opportunity to advise parents and teachers to reinforce these early Stage Six hooks as much as possible. It's indeed a great moment at any time in your life when you're able break out of the pack and believe in yourself enough to use your innate gifts to the fullest.

Since your main obstacles to life at Stage Six are your problematic hooks in the lower stages, the more you believe that you must be what you *can* be, the less likely you will be to let anything or anyone bring you down to the lower stages by pulling on those hooks. Nevertheless, you may sometimes feel a need to react to certain situations or people as you would have when you were operating in those lower stages. This is also fine, as long as it's your choice.

As a Six, you can compartmentalize tasks and even people much more easily. For example, no matter how much passion and enthusiasm might govern your work, you may still have to fill out time and expense reports (Stage Five), flatter a difficult boss or client (Stage Four), follow rules that seem anachronistic (Stage Three), demagogue about an issue (Stage Two), or even at times act powerless (Stage One). Then once the matter that's pulling you down is addressed, it will become second nature to return to Stage Six as your default. This becomes an automatic process, to the extent that you have done the necessary hardwiring.

Thus at Stage Six you are no longer a passenger. You are no longer under the emotional control of others you depend on, your roles, your fears and anxieties, those whose approval you seek, or even your own ego. Your integrity and sense of self are strong enough to overpower all of these things. That now makes you the driver. Your own embedded values are far stronger than what anyone could ever tell you your values should be. Rather than merely being the actor acting out your roles, you are now also the director overseeing and choosing them.

This is why at Stage Six, when you find yourself troubled, confused, or in conflict, you are best served by whatever practice you use to direct yourself inward in order to discover and choose the answer that's right for you. You now know in your mind, your heart, and your gut where to find the strongest source of true wisdom for living your life.

Authority at Stage Six means being *authoritative*, that is, someone people *choose* to look up to, admire, and follow. Sixes admire authoritativeness, but not authoritarianism, which is Stage Three leadership, using rank, force, and fear. The best way to motivate your Stage Six subordinates—if you are in a position to do so—is to give them a challenge that motivates them intrinsically, that activates their passion, creativity, and the synergy that results from them. Then leave them alone to work their magic!

Here a few Stage Six luminaries with whom we are all familiar: Thomas Edison, Isaac Newton, Galileo, Johannes Gutenberg, Jonas Salk, Shakespeare, Michelangelo, Plato, Mozart, Beethoven, George and Ira Gershwin, Madame Curie, Louis Pasteur, Charles Darwin, Christopher Columbus, the Wright Brothers, Alexander Graham Bell, Steve Jobs, Walt Disney, Picasso, Louis Armstrong, Frank Sinatra, Babe Ruth, and Muhammad Ali. As a songwriter, Cole Porter was certainly a Six, but he started out as a lawyer and as he described that career, it was characterized much more by stages Three, Four, and Five. Most entrepreneurs, professional athletes, entertainers, innovators, and countless others who display passion along with joy in pursuing their fields with excellence are members of this club.

The icons mentioned above made gigantic contributions to a world that long survived them, but the Stage

Six club is open to everyone. You are operating at Stage Six whenever you take full charge of your life by listening to, trusting, and, most importantly, acting on your own unique inner resources, just as these giants did. This is the formula you can depend on for reaching your highest potential in any area of your life.

Sixes still feel their own brand of emotional pain. Becoming too attached to your passions and purpose can create suffering when you're surrounded by those operating from the lower stages. You may feel conflicted between your obligations and loyalties to these people and to serving your own higher purpose.

Sixes also sometimes tend to lose balance in their lives because of excessive preoccupation with one area of life, such as their careers, to the exclusion of others, such as family relationships. Many luminaries of all stripes have regretted neglecting their families or even failing to tend to their own health issues until it was too late.

At Stage Six, the choice and ability to both love what you do and do what you love is there for the taking. The roles you now choose to take on will most likely be passion-driven and in your long-term best interest, or chances are you will discard them as quickly as possible. If you have to choose between success and inner peace, most likely you will conclude that inner peace—another staple of the target stages—trumps success.

Living Your Passions:
Strengthening Everything Stage Six

> *"Dream as though you'll live forever.*
> *Live as though you'll die today."*
> —James Dean

That is a great summary of Stage Six!

Living Your Passions: Strengthening Stage Six

What's money? A man is a success if he gets up in the morning and goes to bed at night and in between does what he wants to do.
—BOB DYLAN

Unlike in the five lower stages, we don't focus on climbing out of Stage Six. Instead our mission is to widen, deepen, and strengthen this stage as much as possible. Going beyond Stage Six will be addressed in the next chapter.

Here are eleven strategies and action steps you can take to quickly enter and thrive in this zone of your highest potential. Please look these over and put those that speak to you into your life:

1. Try this Stage Six reflection exercise. If all things were possible, *what would you do with your life right now?* After you have answered this question for today, try to project ahead to next week, next month, next year, five years, twenty years, and finally to the end of your life. Pretend that you can see yourself in those future times and look "back." How would you answer this question for today, from the perspective of each of these different eras?

2. Make a list of times when you were at your absolute best—at peak performance, feeling the best about yourself, strong, successful, unstoppable, and full of passion. Select one of the times you just listed—perhaps the one you consider most powerful. Close your eyes and relive that moment. Allow yourself to reexperience the feelings and the glory associated with it. See the sights, smell the smells, and hear the sounds while you reexperience that feeling of having arrived as fully as possible. Then open your eyes. Observe the body language, breath, thoughts, and facial expressions that go with the experience that you just relived. This is your mind and body in a peak state—your zone of passion. It is something that you can trigger at will. It is also part of your natural frame of mind at Stage Six. You can access it anytime by setting your intention and changing your body language accordingly, and the more you do it, the more natural it will feel. Eventually this state will come to you automatically.

3. If you could be in the peak state you just identified—body language and all—what would you most like to tackle right now? Use this peak state as a foot in the door for what you are most passionate about. I strongly suggest you do it often; think of it as exercising a muscle you'd like to make stronger.

4. If you were beyond money—a billionaire who had all the time in the world to pursue your dream—what would you do differently with your life? (Focus on what you would do after the big trips and the spending sprees are over.) In addition, what would you do differently if you were completely in control of your destiny? Make a list of whatever comes to mind. No doubt you have listed items that are impossible to do without resources that are not yet available to you. So when your list is complete, circle those things you could actually accomplish with your present resources. Chances are there are some passions you can enjoy right now and build on, so go for that low-hanging fruit. Imagine yourself having reached your goals and doing whatever you would be doing when this level of success is at hand. This is the frame of mind that best programs you to succeed.

5. What are your strongest talents? Dare to identify what you are the *best in the world* at. There is probably *something* or some things. Allow yourself to own it or them. Make

another list: "If I were to do only what I believe I was the best at, I would _____." Make that list as long as possible.

6. Make a list of the things you are most likely to be doing when you are feeling the best about yourself. Make another list, of the people you are around when you feel best about yourself. These are the people and things that help bring out the Six in you.

7. Spend a set amount of time, such as one full day (adjust the amount of time up or down to suit yourself), doing only what you associate with your strongest feelings of passion. Take special note of how it feels.

8. Having quality mentors can be the difference between success and failure. If you could have any mentor in the world (either who is alive today or who has ever lived), who would that be? Take a current dilemma or situation you are now dealing with. Write a short essay—even a paragraph or two—on how that person would advise you to resolve your issue. What do these virtual mentors believe about your circumstances that you would be much better off believing? (For example, "this 'impossible' goal is not only attainable, but fun to tackle.") You can have as many of these mentors as you want for different aspects of your life. You can think of these virtual mentors as your strongest

Virtual Mentors

If you could have any mentor in the world,
who would that person or those people be?

Take a current dilemma or situation you are
considering or with which you are now struggling.

Write a short essay on how that virtual
mentor would handle or advise you to
handle or resolve your issue or dilemma.

This is the voice of your "strongest
self" or highest potential.

---

self, or even as the escorts, ushering you to your best life, which you can access twenty-four hours a day.

9. Now back to reality. Is there an *actual* mentor, coach, or therapist who in fact *is* available to you for help in manifesting your dream or removing obstacles to it? The best mentors are generally people who have accomplished and are still accomplishing for themselves what you are now striving to do. Consider accessing the help you need to get moving—now or as soon as possible—as an important step in your Stage Climbing process. Remember, time is the one commodity that cannot be replaced once it's gone.

10. Because the most powerful guidance you seek resides inside of yourself, it's crucial to establish a regular practice to tap into this precious resource. Examples include regular meditation; yoga; long, quiet, reflective walks; visualization and journeying; or a combination of these. They all provide excellent tools to deepen your conscious connection with your inner core. There are numerous sources of information available to help you develop and enhance these practices. Some of the best books, as well as places where meditation and other practices are taught, can be found at StageClimbing.com/resource.

To get you started, mindfulness meditation is easy to learn. Sit comfortably in a chair with both feet on the ground, close your eyes, and gently focus your attention on your breathing, without trying to change how you breathe in any way. Focus on your nostrils or your diaphragm for the in breath and on your mouth, diaphragm, or stomach for the out breath. Do this for a set period of time. If you haven't meditated before, start with a five-minute session daily, then increase your sessions by five minutes each week, until you are at somewhere between twenty and thirty minutes per session. Do one or two sessions daily as time and your willingness permits. Simply stay in the present moment while being still, centered, grounded, and nonjudgmental, while following your natural breath as a guide. Whenever

Mindfulness Meditation Technique

Sit comfortably in a chair with both feet on the ground, close your eyes, and gently focus all of your attention on your breathing without trying to change how you breathe in any way.

Focus on your nostrils or your diaphragm for the *in breath* and your mouth, diaphragm, or stomach for the *out breath*.

It's that simple!

you are aware of your mind taking you in another direction, simply let go of the thought and then gently bring your concentration back to your breathing. Do this while being fully receptive—but not attached—to whatever comes up for you. Thoughts and distractions are a normal part of the practice. Just notice them when they come up, and then return the focus to your breath. This takes some practice, but is well worth it both in the short run and over time. For many years, I personally have done this practice for twenty-five minutes twice daily. It's returned more dividends than I had ever imagined when I began.

There are many other meditation techniques you can use as well. You can learn about some at StageClimbing.com/resources. A regular meditation practice will reward you incredibly with short- and long-term benefits to your health and an increase in well-being, inner peace, clarity of thought, intuition, wisdom, and connection to your higher self.

Here are some additional questions to ask yourself, reflect on, and make lists of the answers for: "What truly inspires me?" "What comes easiest to me?" "What special talents do I have that I am most proud of?" "What rewards do I find to be most gratifying?" Eliminate the rewards and motivations that come from outside of yourself, such as praise or money. Focus instead on your intrinsic rewards or on those that come from within, such as a sense of satisfaction or peace.

What are you willing to do in order to live your unique passion and your purpose-driven life? What trade-offs would you have to make? What is still holding you back? Where do you go from here? No matter what steps you ultimately choose to take, you owe it to yourself to know what your choices are. Most importantly, empower yourself by acknowledging that it is the choices you have made up to now that have led to your life circumstances today. Take complete responsibility for them. Then simply refuse to blame yourself or anyone or anything else for an aspect of your life that you don't like. If you can do this, you have taken a giant step toward gaining control over any remaining toxic hooks. The same can be said for what your circumstances will be tomorrow. You can think of these as the result of today's choices as well as your reward for today's hard work.

Imagine

Life at Stage Seven...

Where we are *beyond self-gratification* and are now ready to use our considerable energies and passions toward a *purpose or mission* that benefits the larger world!

Now imagine that you can take the initiatives you want in all the important areas of life, and imagine you have the self-discipline you need, along with a well-developed conscience and a penchant for living by your own rules. Your life is managed well, and all necessities are provided. As a bonus, you now enjoy what you are doing, so that you are "in joy" with the aspects of life that matter most to you. Could there be anywhere else to go? Yes! You can still raise the bar to make the best you can be even better.

At Stage Seven, we are beyond self-gratification. We are now ready to use our energies and passions on behalf of a mission that benefits the larger world.

CHAPTER NINE

Stage Seven
When Benevolence Takes Over

We make a living by what we get,
but we make a life by what we give.
—Sir Winston Churchill

What would you like your legacy to be? What impact would you most like to leave on the world? On your community? Your favorite cause? The people who matter to you the most?

If it we did not hear a calling to make a greater contribution, living our lives at Stage Six would be all we could ever want. Our only remaining challenge would be to find more ways to gratify ourselves in order to enjoy life even more. For many people, this is indeed all they need or want. But fortunately for our civilization, as our passions evolve, they tend to take us in other directions. We have Stage Seven—the highest stage—which expands that zone of our potential to take us beyond ourselves. The biggest distinction between stages Six and Seven is that at Stage

Seven your focus shifts away from yourself and outwardly toward the world that's greater than you.

At Stage Seven, the forces of gratitude and passion work together. The result: you are simply no longer as motivated by the personal rewards of Stage Six. They're still nice to have, but at Stage Seven, what's in it for you alone no longer inspires or satisfies you as it once did. You hear a new calling to give something back. As the ancient Chinese proverb reminds us, "One generation plants the trees; another gets the shade."

Ironically, at Stage Seven your own personal enjoyment is optional. Sevens keep the world going by their realization that there's only so much they can keep for themselves.

Many at Stage Six find that they've become victims of their own success, when things that used to motivate them no longer do. Sometimes it's merely boredom (one of our most underrated stressors) that tells you it's time to redirect your focus. Some Sixes actually burn out on their own gratification, then realize that something more is needed to bring meaning back to their lives.

Stage Seven seems to be the natural and logical answer. Alan, the businessman you met in the last chapter, came to recognize that his mission now was to start a foundation devoted to bringing his company's services to impoverished areas of the country. This fired up his passion and obliterated his depression. This Stage Seven solution was what he needed. In his case, treating the depression alone would

Stage Seven:
Second of Two Target Steps

Stage Seven is the highest stage attainable. At Stage Seven, *you're beyond needing self-gratification!*

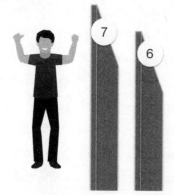

✦ You find fulfillment as a result of your benevolence and your purpose driven unique contribution to others, to the world, and to how you can be an agent of change in some large or small way.

✦ Your purpose outside of yourself has more importance to you than what is purely in your own self-interest.

have amounted to little more than a cover-up. I could give you many examples of cases like Alan's, but I would rather focus on how it could best apply to *your* life.

Your ultimate goal at Stage Seven is to change the world in some way, large or small, by having the greatest possible impact where you think it matters most, such as helping a person or a cause you believe in. For many, this is where goodness morphs into greatness, and there is no limit to where it can all lead. In this process there still *is* something in it for you—an unmistakable level of satisfaction, connected to a bigger purpose, that the stages below Seven simply couldn't deliver.

To the extent that you operate as a Seven, personal success is no longer your issue. You've transcended thinking in terms of your own success and failure. You've broken out of that pack. In Stage Climbing, this is the ultimate personal success.

Sevens instinctively understand this simple paradox, which is the key to happiness: by focusing on your own happiness, you rarely achieve it in a lasting way; but by helping someone else—or many others—happiness and fulfillment come back to you almost effortlessly. Those you help can be individuals, groups, organizations, or nations. They can be close family members, neighbors, friends, animals, the environment, those you remember in your will that may never have the chance to thank you, people you have never met and never will, the entire world, or any segment of it. The desire to help is what all Sevens have in common. It is only the mission and the recipients that vary.

Just as in Stage Six, all the guidance you need ultimately resides within you. In both Stages Six and Seven, you are internally directed and motivated. That's what makes them similar. And you can access the source of this information and motivation by whatever means you use to go inward and self-reflect, as discussed in the last chapter. Often the right spiritual guide, role model, or mentor can also be helpful to you in this process.

Whenever you are helping someone who can't reciprocate, and with no strings attached, you are operating out of Stage Seven. As always, your purpose is a highly individual matter. For some, helping one person is enough. For others, nothing short of changing the entire world will do. Your contribution can range from giving time or money that you can easily afford to giving your life, or anything in between. It's not the size of your mission that's important. It's simply the true desire to give back. Any cause you connect with or contribution that you make can be considered a Stage Seven endeavor as long as it's not merely out of obligation, for financial rewards, or for any of the other reasons that are staples of the lower stages.

Our collective hooks to Stage Seven keep this planet going. The Stage Seven club is open to you at any age and in any area of your life. Any act of selflessness can be your ticket. If, at the age of ten, you worked hard to sell Girl Scout Cookies for all the right reasons, or you risked your popularity at school by befriending someone unpopular without regard to how you would be viewed by your peers, you probably did so as a result of an early Stage Seven hook. In fact, whether or not you realize it, there are probably many ways you're there already. For example, donating blood—unless you're merely doing it to fit in or get praise—is a Stage Seven hook in action.

Good parenting that's grounded in love, where you genuinely put your child's needs above your own, is certainly one of the most common and universal Stage Seven endeavors. Most parents routinely make incalculable sacrifices of time, money, and perhaps their own ambitions when raising children, and not merely because they "should."

This also holds true when you take care of siblings, aging parents, or other family members with special needs. Of course, the assumption is that your true motives are not from the lower stages, such as out of guilt (Stage Three) or in order to receive praise or love in return (Stage Four).

Another example is mentoring someone when even a small amount of your time could enable him or her to find a healthy path in life. Can you think of anyone who might have made that kind of difference in your life?

A Stage Seven act that requires little sacrifice could be merely sending a blessing, a meditation, or a prayer to a person or cause that could use some positive or healing energy. Stage Seven also involves ordinary people anonymously helping other ordinary people, for example, picking up a piece of glass on the beach that is not likely to hurt you, yet might have cut the next person walking by. Helping a blind person with a simple task, or reaching out to an isolated and elderly neighbor—one who has no one else and perhaps nothing to give you back—are but a couple of other examples of the infinite range of Stage Seven contributions. In the next chapter, there will be many examples of Stage Seven acts as compared to those of the other stages.

Your hooks are highly personal matters. As in Stage Six, at Stage Seven, how you feel about yourself regarding your activities is a great litmus test. You can easily fool others as to whether or not your acts are genuine, but what's in your heart is accessible only by you. You know your motives. For instance, if you've sacrificed your own financial comfort to provide for your children's college education, have you done so in order for them to owe you, or out of a fear that otherwise they will not take care of you in your old age (Stage One)? In order to gain access to a trust fund that a grandparent set up for your child, where your real agenda is to net more money for yourself than you actually put out (Stage Two)? Because you would otherwise feel guilty, since a rule has been drilled into you saying that only bad parents don't pay for college (Stage Three)? So that your children will love you, praise you, and show you gratitude for their subsequent success (Stage Four)? Because it's simply a part of the parents' role to help their children reap the rewards of a college education (Stage Five)? Did you do it as a way of demonstrating your feelings of joy and parental love (Stage Six)? Or in order to see them benefit, enhance their ability to contribute to the world, and trigger the many ripple effects that their subsequent contributions will make (Stage Seven)? Of course, there can be an infinite combination of reasons and motives in play.

At Stage Seven, you never need to be thanked, appreciated, or given anything in return. Your contribution is based on your own intention regarding the greater good it will do. You may, for example, express your gratitude toward someone who once helped you by helping someone else who needs it now.

Contribution to a charity or cause is similar. Your true motive tells the story. At Stage Seven, you may be inspired to benefit the world or promote a cause you believe in. You expect nothing in return; at times your contribution could even make your own life more complicated or difficult. At Stage Six, you may be motivated by the opportunity to do some type of work that you enjoy doing that you don't have the chance to do as a part of your regular life. At Stage Five, it could be to fulfill the expected role of giving back (and besides, giving to charity may be tax-deductible). At Stage Four, it could be to receive the praise and recognition that often comes as a result of giving. Many charities even publish the names of their donors partially for that purpose. (Closet Sevens are often listed as "Anonymous.") Another way to put it is that Fours (as well as Twos) can act like Sevens when the cameras are rolling. At Stage Three, you may be giving merely to stay out of hell; at Stage Two, to convince others that you have pure intentions, so that they will fall prey to a scam of yours; and at Stage One, in order to somehow actually receive that charity's help. Once again, infinite combinations from all seven stages are possible.

At Stage Seven, you can now understand the motives of those you have passed along the way. Just remember that they might not be able to understand yours. Even more importantly, the higher you go, the more you can understand yourself and how you operated at your lower stages. Accept this insight as a gift. Reflect on why you may have done or thought certain things during earlier, less evolved times of your life. This knowledge is invaluable for managing your hooks, letting go of the past, and staying on your chosen path.

For example, at Stage Seven you are no longer internally guided by shoulds or absolutes. At Stages One and Two, you may still need them to survive. At Stage Three, you generally agree with them, while at Stage Four you try to fight them, but often lose. At Stage Five, you finally start winning the battle of the shoulds, but they're still a force in your life to be reckoned with until you climb to Stages Six and Seven.

Unlike those at lower stages, Sevens tend never to ask for or expect any more respect or love from someone else than they are willing to give. This applies to your children and subordinates as well as to everyone else in your world. You now know that treating others with respect sets an example and is synergistic. Nevertheless, you can also accept the fact that it only comes back to you as strongly as the other person is capable of sending it. Even if that person is unable or unwilling to reciprocate, it is not a problem for you. You now understand that if you have self-respect, you don't really need validation from others in order to feel worthwhile (although it still feels good to receive it at any stage.).

At Stage Seven, you've raised the bar. You can certainly continue to grow, expand, and change, but there are no higher stages to aspire to. Since your own personal gratification and fulfillment no longer require much of your attention, you are now emotionally freer and more able to put your energy into your higher calling. No longer are you painfully needy or self-absorbed. You are finished with the type of self-destructive behavior that caused you innumerable problems in the past. Any remaining self-doubts will rarely stand up to what you have chosen as your mission. You have developed a reservoir of inner resources and wisdom to live life at the highest levels of consciousness.

As a Seven, your preferred reaction to conflict is to listen to and consider the views of view of everyone concerned, including you. Because you seek no absolute realities and are no longer governed by rigid or obsolete rules, you understand that others have their own points of view as well, no matter how radically different they may be. That certainly doesn't mean you buy into them, but you will allow them to become part of the larger conversation. You consider each possibility, then make the decision that best serves everyone involved. The preferable result is to find consensus. If this is not possible, you will staunchly stand by your decision or action, based on the principles that underlie it. (Principles are internally generated by you, whereas rigid and obsolete rules are *not*.)

Now you not only have a much greater capacity for empathy, but can also appreciate the role empathy plays in your mission. For example, a tragedy, such as the death of your child, could trigger a wide range of responses. At Stage One, you could become emotionally paralyzed by feelings of grief and victimhood. At Stage Seven, however, you might devote time and money to saving other parents from the same experience by battling the condition or circumstances that led to the tragedy. You can apply this principle to virtually any life challenge.

Your cause can become even more important to you than your own physical or emotional well-being. In other words, at Stage Seven, your purpose can actually overtake yourself. Many Sevens would relinquish their own wealth and personal comfort if they conflicted with their mission. Examples include those who choose lives of pure service, such as nuns, priests, monks, and even those serving dangerous missions in the military. Such people are able to put aside practically every other aspect of life—material and otherwise—on behalf of service.

Certainly this level of dedication is not required at Stage Seven, and in fact it is an option that only a small percentage of people exercise. Much more typical is a tendency to do what you know is the right thing instead of what's easier or more popular. This would come naturally to a Stage Seven politician—ignoring polls and other pressures that summon up their stages Two, Three, Four, and

Five hooks. Most notably, you are secure enough within yourself to commit to taking what Robert Frost described as "the road less traveled" (also the title of a best seller by M. Scott Peck) and focus instead on the world you will leave behind.

Spirituality at Stage Seven is tightly connected to your mission, and to varying degrees drives it. Your dialogue with God or a higher consciousness (as you define them) is uniquely personal. As in Stage Six, you access your spiritual guidance by whatever means you find best. But at Stage Seven, you may even go a step further by asking how you can bring this higher consciousness to any situation or conflict you are facing.

Many ponder the mystery of life after death. This is one of the many secrets that the universe and the divine do indeed withhold. At Stage Seven, you are comfortable with whatever conclusion you reach about this great mystery. But you also realize that although it is natural to contemplate the afterlife, the ultimate reality—which, perhaps by design, is not knowable with certainty—is not that important, since you remain keenly focused on this life, and you would probably not live it any differently no matter what you believed.

Here are some other examples of Stage Seven spiritual principles and beliefs that are often part of most custom blends:

- "Laws of spirit apply equally to all of us" (for example, "we are all one"; "ultimately our cores all want the same thing"; "we each have a unique purpose"; "karmic rewards and consequences apply to all actions we take").
- "Everything happens for a reason."
- "Those who act badly do so because they've lost their way."
- "We achieve solace from God by helping and serving others, even our adversaries."
- "Enlightenment is never completely achieved in this lifetime."
- "Spirituality and perhaps even immortality are intertwined with living and accomplishing your life's purpose."

As a Seven, your close relationships never have to be limited to those who share your mission, values, or beliefs. Not only can you tolerate those with other points of view, but you have a keen appreciation of them. You can encourage those you love to follow their passion and reach their potential even if it causes you some inconvenience or disappointment.

In marriages and love relationships that operate at Stage Seven, the couple becomes a team that selflessly works together in a common mission outside of themselves (such as raising their children or being active in their community or for a cause). You can easily put your partner first, and you may even put your partner's mission above your own without expecting a quid pro quo. You are beyond attachments to each other's expectations. There's even a Stage Seven attitude about sex, which sees it as a way to deepen the loving connection between partners, sometimes spiritually.

A Stage Seven couple that grows apart will never find the partners putting each other in the wrong in order to justify a breakup. Instead they will have no problem seeing the other person as a being separate from his or her role in the relationship. They will react with gratitude for the good things they had rather than with anger for what the relationship did not provide. Yet it should also be noted that many of the greats in virtually every field have been criticized by their children or spouses as being there for the world, but not for their families. The son of one famous luminary once told me, "I can personally attest to the adage that great men are not necessarily good men." Being a solid Seven in one area of life does not necessarily mean you are operating from that stage in another.

Another difference between Stage Six and Stage Seven is that at Stage Six, the rewards are usually obvious. But at Stage Seven, it's quite possible for you to be the only one to realize the nature or scope of your impact—or perhaps you may not even fully comprehend it yourself.

For many people, including some of the greats throughout history, a Stage Six passion can lead to a Stage

Seven consciousness. For example, after Marconi discovered how to use radio waves, the world was never again the same. It is hard to imagine life today without radio, television, or satellite technology. Nevertheless, he was not the first person to explore the existence of radio waves. Many others before him had that vision but were famously judged to be insane (for hearing voices) or at the very least quite weird.

Indeed, many Sevens have risked or ruined their reputations to pursue their missions. In Marconi's case, despite the scorn, ridicule, and adversity, he had the courage and the genius to bring his vision to full fruition. The difference between people like Marconi and those who keep their "silly" ideas to themselves is part of the definition of Stage Seven. History is full of examples where the "crazy people" of one era are recognized as the visionaries and geniuses in another.

In fact, history's Stage Seven icons and luminaries, at their best, have the same intention you do when you unselfishly donate blood or bone marrow. Perhaps your contribution will save the life of someone who will go on to have a major impact on the world. Like you, those legendary figures could rarely if ever control the outcome of their contribution—only the intentions and the actions they took. It was John D. Rockefeller—the Rockefeller who actually made all of the family's money—who said, "Think of giving not as a duty but as a privilege."

At Stage Seven, you're in good company—among the greatest luminaries and sources of inspiration ever. As we understand the inner workings of some of history's greatest Sevens, for example; Jesus, Moses, Muhammad, Abraham Lincoln, Mahatma Gandhi, Martin Luther King, Mother Teresa, and Joan of Arc, we realize that they were known for listening to their inner voices and following their deepest and strongest convictions. They carried on despite consequences including rejection, ridicule, and giving up the material benefits of life and sometimes even life itself.

True spiritual leaders, saints, mystics, and sages are all examples of those who have operated at Stage Seven. They are rare specimens of humanity. In many cases, they often acquired huge followings with little or no effort on their part. Their very presence has been experienced as something holy. On the other hand, they represented such a threat to their Stage Three contemporaries, who were opposed to their often radical views, that they were sometimes martyred. Many of the greatest Sevens were never in their lifetime to know the impact their contributions would make, but we can assume that to them, the outcome would not have mattered as much as their efforts to manifest what they stood for. What probably kept them going was a rock-solid belief that they were much more than their physical bodies or anything else that is of this world.

Another pivotal factor is intention. Bill Gates's contributions to the world through Microsoft were originally motivated by his Stage Six passion for computers and business (and possibly even a lower-stage hook here and there with regard to business practices). But the enormous wealth he obtained led him subsequently to make unprecedented contributions of time and money through the Bill and Melinda Gates Foundation. Like Warren Buffett, he encourages others of great wealth to do the same. This phase of his transformation clearly makes him a Stage Seven luminary—in addition to being an iconic Six through the work for which he is best-known.

The same is true for Albert Einstein, who famously said, "It is every man's obligation to put back into the world at least the equivalent of what he takes out of it." Einstein's work as a physicist (Stage Six) gave him a giant platform on which to affect our thinking about world peace and to apply his wisdom to many areas outside of physics (Stage Seven). There is no doubt that Oprah Winfrey's show won her praise and prestige (Stage Four), money (Stage Five), and professional satisfaction (Stage Six), but it's what she gives back through her work on behalf of many causes, such as education in Africa, that would cause most of us to think of her as a Seven.

We rarely think of Sevens as being motivated by fun or even by needing to enjoy what they are doing. They do their mission because it needs to be done, and the inspiration for doing it—perhaps felt or understood only by them at the time—along with inner peace and the satisfaction that comes from accomplishment, is characteristically all the reinforcement they need. And often they don't even take the time to savor that!

Most of our Stage Seven contributions seem modest compared to those of the giants, but they are by no means any less important in the grand scheme, when your intention is to serve and your contribution is motivated by benevolence. We all have the power to act on and live by those same convictions. Abraham Lincoln—a charter member of this exalted group—said, "In the end, it's not the years in your life that count, it's the life in your years."

Here are a few more examples of ways you can use or perhaps have used your Stage Seven hooks to leave the world a better place:

- Whenever you put the more pressing needs of your children, aging parents, or other family members or friends above your own, such as by caring for the sick or giving some help financially—out of the desire to help rather than out of obligation.

- Any time you give your time or money to a charitable endeavor without regard to praise, recognition, or any other benefits other than your own satisfaction.

- Putting your reputation on the line or postponing a goal of your own for another person, a mission, or a cause greater than yourself—again, when it's unlikely that you will experience any direct benefits.

- Any disinterested act of random kindness.

- Sacrificing your time to help with a mission you believe in or standing up for underdogs or the underprivileged.
- Reporting a crime with possible backlash.
- Blogging about an injustice.
- Being a whistleblower, especially when it entails negative consequences to yourself, in order to prevent a future injustice.

Often pain is what mobilizes the Seven in you to take definitive action. Anger can morph into determination, which can then be directed toward righting a wrong. At Stage Seven, however, you are able to manage your expectations of people and events so that your anger does not overpower you or block your ability to seek solutions. Sevens are least likely to take things personally, but they tend to be most frustrated when they are—or feel—powerless to right a wrong or carry out their mission. In fact, at Stage Seven, anger can act as a wake-up call, energizing you to take effective and decisive action. Beyond that, it only hurts *you* to feel it. Thus as a Seven you will be unlikely to allow yourself to stew with anger for long. Instead you will probably let go of it once you've gotten and acted on its message.

For Sevens, forgiving those who have deliberately hurt them tends to be a no-brainer. Forgiving and letting go, even though you get nothing in return from the other person, is a Stage Seven event, and for many, the ability to do so is a major breakthrough. As Nelson Mandela said,

"Being angry is like drinking poison, then hoping your enemy will be the one who suffers as a result."

Even at Stage Seven, you most certainly have good and bad days, but you are far past any expectations that life can or should be perfect!

A Perspective on the Target Stages

For many, the rewards of Stage Six are all you could possibly want right now. At Stage Six, you are at the pinnacle of healthy pleasure, and aside from where your Stage Seven hooks naturally take you, there is no place else you may truly want to go. For others, Stage Six takes on that "been there, done that" quality which begs for something more. That new plateau, of course, is often what challenges you to go beyond yourself and enter Stage Seven territory (with a degree of benevolence as your guide). And remember, Stage Seven may be just the ideal stage for you as a parent, spouse, and friend, or in some aspects of your avocations.

You need only listen to the message that comes to you in the form of an intuition, calling, or desire, in whatever way you channel it. Just remember not to mistake a should for a calling (for example, "I feel guilty about all I have, so I *should* give back"). That's still virtuous, but your motivation is at Stage Three, not Stage Seven.

There's a Zen saying: "The wise men said it couldn't be done; the fool then came and did it." Many causes that have one chance in a thousand of reaching fruition would have been seen as too difficult or impossible in any of the lower stages, but at Stage Seven, that one-in-a-thousand (or million, or billion) chance might be the only odds you need to bring passion to some important mission. And when your next mission is ripe, that same inner voice will let you know.

I certainly encourage you to develop more Stage Seven hooks. Rarely if ever will you regret having them. The action steps that follow offer some help in that area.

Going beyond Yourself: Expanding Stage Seven

There's no place to climb to from Stage Seven, only new missions to consider and hooks in the lower stages to manage.

Stage Seven is grounded in the truth you most deeply believe. This is the one characteristic that all of Stage Seven people have in common. So your first job is to be in tune with your truth and faithfully abide by it, wherever it takes you.

If there's a recipe for reaching Stage Seven, it's to let the combination of your passion (to manifest something new) and your gratitude (for what you already have) be the forces that guide you. *Just about all of the Stage Six action steps that focus on accessing your inner resources apply to Stage Seven as well.* Here are a few more things to reflect on:

1. What purpose or purposes outside of yourself inspire you to care deeply? It could be a charitable endeavor, a political issue or candidate, some form of injustice, the environment, an ongoing world problem, or any matter affecting others beyond yourself. Your mission could also be one that benefits a specific person or group—an immediate family member, a complete stranger, or a specific population, such as children or animals, who need some kind of help that you could provide.

2. Identify areas where you could see yourself expending energy toward something outside of you. (In the lower stages you would have called up this energy when you were looking to benefit yourself directly.) What steps are you willing to take to benefit that cause or mission? If nothing comes up, let it go for now, but make it a point to revisit this question from time to time. Trust that a Stage Seven mission with the necessary level of inspiration and motivation will find you when the time is right. Remember: the way in which most Sixes go toward Stage Seven is first by simply listening to their inner dialogue, concerns, and passions, and then by allowing themselves to be guided by them.

3. Expand your practice of meditation, yoga, or other ways of deepening your reservoir of wisdom and insight. Maintain a form of practice as a permanent staple in your life.

4. Visualize the impact on others and the world that your involvement could have. Then notice any fluctuations in your interest or inspiration.

5. Commit yourself in every way possible to your intention to contribute. You may want to do one Stage Seven act per day, per week, or per month. Acts of kindness, charitable contributions of time or money, and any type of community involvement all count.

6. Remember that by supporting and reinforcing someone else's Stage Seven behavior, you are in effect operating as a Seven yourself. You can take this simple step at any time, by contributing whatever time, money, or other resources you wish, to a mission you believe in that's being championed by another committed person.

In the next chapter, we will explore what it would mean to operate at Stage Seven as well as all of the seven stages, in many selected aspects of your life.

CHAPTER TEN

Calibrating Your Stage Climb
The Shortest Path from Where You Are Now to Where You Want to Be

In the previous chapters, we focused on each of the seven stages separately. Now it's time to look at your Stage Climbing process across all seven stages. This is a powerful way of putting it all together and actually observing some results.

A calibration is a type of measurement that's designed to fine-tune or pinpoint something with as much precision as possible. In Stage Climbing, I use the term *calibration* as a metaphor for determining the precise stage at which you are operating now, so that you can establish exactly where you want to be in a given area of your life.

This chapter contains numerous life applications and examples that encompass all seven stages. In a specific area, you can now see how life at any given stage compares with the other stages. Remember, the seven stages represent a choice of seven lenses that are available to you through which to view any aspect of your life. Use these calibrations to reflect upon these areas and tweak them into insights, attitudes, and goals that fit you exactly.

As you look at each page in this chapter, *begin at the stage you most identify with.* Stage Five is a good starting point for whenever this is unclear to you, since it's generally the most neutral or dispassionate stage. *Then identify where you want to be.*

The lower stages can also be seen as reminders of how you used to be, such as during a prior marriage or relationship; when you chose your line of work; or how you were raised. They can also provide you with vivid descriptions of others in your life so that you can relate to them on their own turf. In some cases, looking at these lower-stage calibrations can be a wake-up call, or perhaps it could be the first step toward self-acceptance in that part of your life.

Think of the higher-stage calibrations (Stages Six and Seven) as a rough draft of your potential or personal goals. In some areas of your life, you may already be where you want to be, while other areas cry out to you for change. Stage Seven usually includes many of the best elements of Stage Six as well as certain unique characteristics of its own.

Use these calibrations as needed to pick a new attitude or view of life. After pondering all the stages in a given category, you may find it helpful to write down your goals and continue to tweak them until they fit you and your life situation exactly. To help keep yourself on track, refer to your goals often until they become second nature. The appendix offers the complete strategy to help you do that. At StageClimbing.com/calibrations, you will find many more calibrations that could not be included here. We are adding more all the time.

Think of climbing the stages as rising to those occasions of life you most cherish. Once you know where you are and where you want to go, relentlessly commit to doing whatever it takes to live by your choices and get there!

Your Ultimate Master Goals

This first calibration looks at your Ultimate Master Goals, which are different at each stage. Here they are, broken down by the stages. See which of these speak most to various parts of your life and how you can best implement the ones you choose:

Stage Seven. To change the world or some part of it in some way, large or small. To have the greatest possible impact on those around you, as well as on any cause with which you involve yourself.

Stage Six. To do what you love, are best at, and enjoy most. To strive to fill your particular niche as well as it could possibly be done—in your own unique way and for your own intrinsic pleasure. To love what you do and the people who matter most to you. To operate at your highest potential.

Stage Five. To have affluence. To have whatever you believe is necessary for living a good and worthwhile life, as well as having all of your roles optimally covered and comfortably balanced.

Stage Four. To be accepted, admired, and loved by those who matter to you, perhaps even regardless of whether or not you actually know them personally.

Stage Three. To be conflict-free.

Stage Two. To get exactly what you want and have fun while avoiding scrutiny, punishment, or other consequences.

Stage One. To have all your needs met with minimal effort or obligation on your part.

Be especially aware of whether or not you are putting energy into seeking what you really don't want or no longer need—perhaps merely by habit. If so, where could that energy better serve you now?

The Stages You Are Operating At

To determine the stage at which you are operating in a specific life area or situation, ask yourself the questions next to the stage they typify. If more than one seems to resonate, simply be aware of which stage you relate to the most for this aspect of life:

Stage Seven. Are the needs of all others in this situation or big picture *at least as* important to me as my own needs? (In addition to the questions for Stage Six below.)

Stage Six. Am I doing what I feel passionate about? What feels right, ethical, and best to me on a heartfelt level? Are my best feelings about myself being triggered?

Stage Five. Am I taking into account those things that affect all aspects of my life, and the roles in it that I play?

Stage Four. Am I being influenced or governed by what others who have no authority over me think of me?

Stage Three. Am I insisting that there is only one way or one set of rules or beliefs that both I and everyone else involved should follow?

Stage Two. Am I trying to get away with something, reap a reward I am not entitled to, or do something that would be objectionable if someone else were doing it to me? On the unproblematic side, is this just sheer uninhibited fun?

Stage One. Do I believe I am too dependent, helpless, or weak to take the initiative to do what needs to be done? Am I telling myself I am powerless? Am I being just plain resistant to taking measures that I know would benefit me?

Conflict Management

Here is how conflict is typically handled at each stage:

Stage Seven. By carefully listening to all points of view, considering each possibility, and making the decision that comes closest to best serving everyone, by consensus if possible. Then by staunchly standing by your decision or action if necessary. (In addition to the questions for Stage Six and possibly Stage Five below).

Stage Six. By doing what feels consistent with your own core principles and purpose on a heartfelt level.

Stage Five. By evaluating how the source of your conflict is related to your bigger picture, then by taking the action that come as close as possible to rebalancing your life.

Stage Four. By taking the road that produces the most validation from others and the least anxiety, no matter how things shake out.

Stage Three. By following a set of black-and-white rules that clearly dictates who or what is right and who or what is wrong.

Stage Two. By using some form of deception or strong-arm tactic or doing whatever you have to do to make sure you get your way. To get what you want at Stage Two, you might be extremely charming to manipulate others, or extremely brutal to bully, manipulate, or force them (or any combination thereof). Doing whatever it takes to control, overpower, and win.

Stage One. By doing what is easiest, such as latching on to some person or force that you consider more capable and letting them take over the situation, thus disowning any conflict by obeying them and supporting their means of resolving the conflict.

A comprehensive menu for conflict resolution might even include something from *each* stage. The key is to choose the most effective approach or combination of them for a given situation or issue. In reality, most of us use our hooks in all or several stages at different times to resolve conflict.

Defining Happiness and Success

This is how you would define happiness and success at each stage:

Stage Seven. Achieving the desired impact on a person or people that you most care about. Helping others and seeing them reap the benefits of your efforts. Being fully engaged in your principles and purpose.

Stage Six. The satisfaction of reaching a difficult goal or solving a tough problem. The feelings of excitement and triumph that comes from peak performance. The bliss and inner peace associated with the little things in everyday life, such as the glow of a nice spring day, writing poetry, reading a good book, or listening to your favorite music. Exploring novelty and whatever makes you curious. Being with those you love and feeling deeply connected to them.

Stage Five. Keeping all roles and relationships in balance and problem-free. Being effective and not overwhelmed. Achieving affluence. Finding a hobby and making time for pleasurable activities in order to balance your life and recharge your batteries. Engaging in activities that provide fun and offer a healthy alternative to work and chores.

Stage Four. Achieving acceptance, approval, fame, and positive recognition. Winning an award. Keeping personal relationships happy and conflict-free.

Stage Three. Living your life "properly" by staying within the black-and-white parameters of your accepted world. Not drawing any negative attention to yourself. Fitting in and doing what you "should" as well as doing your part to make others toe the line. The belief that your religious or spiritual path, and yours alone, is most in tune with the divine.

Stage Two. Getting away with something or achieving dominance over people. On the positive side, sheer joy and a lack of unwanted inhibition.

Stage One. When life is easy with no demands or challenges to worry about. Having a reliable and dependable caretaker who provides all necessities.

The best thing about Stages Six and Seven is that they put your happiness and success firmly under *your* control. This is what makes your stage climb so empowering!

Motivation

What motivates you at each stage:

Stage Seven. The opportunity to serve others, your larger community, or the environment in a cause you believe in. To solve a problem that has an impact on people or things that are larger than you and your inner circle. The satisfaction of either touching one life (as a parent, for example) or bettering many lives.

Stage Six. The feeling of satisfaction that comes from doing what you love and were meant to do as indicated by your unique talents. Meeting a challenge. Performing optimally, with passion and ease. Anything that triggers feelings of bliss. Being genuinely creative. Feeling the best about yourself. As the saying goes, "If you aren't having fun doing it, either you're not doing it right or it's not the right thing for you to be doing."

Stage Five. Money, benefits, privileges, respect from others for specific aspects of your life or specific roles you play (such as that of a manager). Handling your roles and responsibilities. Having all chores and obligations under control.

Stage Four. Awards, celebrity, prestige, validation, praise, love, recognition, and approval (globally as opposed to in some specific area of life, as in Stage Five). The opportunity to impress friends, acquaintances, colleagues, relatives, or the public.

Stage Three. Not making waves. Doing whatever is expected of you and staying on the good side of authority. Having the power to rule others.

Stage Two. Reaping rewards without paying the necessary dues or playing on a level field. Being irresponsible while avoiding consequences.

Stage One. Whatever feels easiest, safest, least threatening, and most comfortable.

Whenever I speak on motivation or coach managers about motivating subordinates, I emphasize that motivation is never a "one size fits all" process. Whether you are simply trying to nail down what motivates you or you are trying to motivate others, it's crucial to understand the stage from which you or they are starting.

In most cases, Stages Six and Seven appear quite appealing, as long as you or those you are motivating remember that it's still also OK to strive for lower-stage or external motivators such as money and recognition. The highest stages will always offer the bonuses of personal satisfaction, enjoying what you do, and contributing to something larger than yourself.

Problem Solving

To solve problems, here is where you would typically turn for help at each stage:

Stage Seven. A spiritual master of some type who helps you to transcend your ego and access your inner resources. Meditation, prayer, yoga, journaling, journeying, or any method that works for you to turn inward for guidance.

Stage Six. A well-chosen mentor or coach who is in the arena where you need help and who is personally beyond the challenge you are struggling with. Many of the same practices as for Sevens (see above) that connect you with your inner resources, such as meditation.

Stage Five. Self-help books (such as this one), courses, and audio and video programs. Talking to people you value. Peers and peer groups that focus on personal growth or on a specific challenge you are trying to meet.

Stage Four. Psychotherapy for treatment of anxiety, depression, anger, low self-esteem, or relationship conflicts. But be aware that sometimes psychotherapy amounts to little more than a kind of prostituted friendship, so pick your therapist carefully. Choose one with an approach that emphasizes results and has you working in between sessions to integrate the results into your life in the shortest time possible.

Stage Three. The Bible or some other sacred book, a church, a clergyperson, or a charismatic leader who clearly spells out the rules that you need to follow in order to resolve the issue. On the more positive side: an exception or loophole in a rule you believe you must follow, or someone (a creditable friend, family member, clergyperson, or therapist) to help you move to a new way of thinking.

Stage Two. Legal counsel. Behavior modification and other concrete forms of counseling to change errant habits that threaten relationships or freedom.

Stage One. Someone you see as more capable than you are to take over and allow you to resume a conflict-free existence. Medication or drug detoxification for medical and certain emotional issues.

In my practice, I have seen many—sometimes heartbreaking—examples of how people have suffered far longer and more severely than they had to simply because they were not receiving the type of support that could most effectively help them resolve their issue.

Therefore a main function of this book is to enable you to choose the right sources of help. The strategies in this book and discussions in each chapter offer resources that can be most helpful on a stage-by-stage basis. Additional resources can be found at StageClimbing.com/resources.

Calibrations for Your Essential Areas of Life

These next seven calibrations are meant to put some of the essential areas of your life into perspective. They include calibrations for your career, job and career changes, spirituality and families, love relationships and marriages, and parenting both from the perspective of the child and the parent. Each of these calibrations could easily be the subject of a book of its own. But here are the essentials.

Work and Career

These are the typical *best* attitudes about your career and the work you do by the stages:

> **Stage Seven.** "It's an excellent way (or the best way I can) to make the contribution I most want to make."

> **Stage Six.** "I love what I do. It's what comes easiest to me, feels most flowing and natural. I wouldn't want to be doing anything else. I feel fulfilled irrespective of the financial and other extrinsic rewards I get. I get pleasure from the challenge of it. If I never again *had* to work, I would still choose to be doing this."

Stage Five. "It's lucrative (or pays the bills). It gives me something to do. It has nice contacts and perks."

Stage Four. "It gives me prestige. I get a steady stream of good people contact."

Stage Three. "It is the type of work my family 'tribe' does (or always did) or values most."

Stage Two. "It gives me opportunities to feel powerful by manipulating and bullying others. It's a way to make easy money."

Stage One. "It's safe and provides me with feelings of security."

If you cannot identify with stages Six and Seven above in terms of your career, you may want to consider this page a wake-up call. I have met very few people who couldn't find a way to operate at least out of Stage Six with respect to some major aspect of their careers if they really wanted to. Although getting there may certainly take a lot of effort, the rewards are immeasurable! The next section takes this concept a step further.

Job Changes

Typical reasons for making job or career changes:

Stage Seven. To move on to serve another or a higher mission.

Stage Six. To seek a greater, more fulfilling, or a more enjoyable personal challenge, where you are doing what you love and really want to spend your precious time doing it.

Stage Five. For advancement, more money, fewer hours, easier commute, better contacts or benefits.

Stage Four. May seek change because of not fitting in with, not getting along with, or not liking or being liked by the boss or coworkers. For more prestige. To follow an emotionally nurturing boss.

Stage Three. Need for more structure or regimentation. (Coworkers get away with too much.) To obtain more power.

Stage Two. You were exposed for violating policy or claiming undeserved credit, or for other forms of illegal or unethical behavior.

Stage One. Job became too challenging or less secure.

You may be aware that a job or career change is necessary for you, but feel stuck. If you currently are nowhere near Stage Six with your work but wish you were, take this opportunity to ponder what you really want to be doing with this part of your life. Make a list of all the excuses that are holding you back and deal with each one separately. Or for the sake of this exercise, *pretend that your excuses simply don't exist. What would you do then?*

I have helped people of all ages and life circumstances to get into careers that were believed to have any roadblock you could think of. In the end, almost anything is possible unless you persist in believing it isn't.

What career or job would put you in Stage Six or Seven? Identify the one or ones that would. Then as a *first step*, get the information you need to begin taking action or at least making the first step. Leave no stone unturned in pursuing your dream. Also, revisit the Stage Six strategies, starting on page 166, as well as all of your other resources, to do what it takes to make this happen.

Spirituality

Your view of spirituality by the stages:

Stage Seven. Sevens characteristically come to and live by their own custom blend of spiritual principles, but the following are usually included: "Laws of spirit apply to all of us" ("We are all one"; "our cores basically want the same thing"; "we each have a unique purpose"; "there are karmic rewards and consequences to consider"). "Those who act badly do so because they lost their way." "We achieve solace with God by helping and serving others, including even our adversaries." "Whether or not there is an afterlife has no bearing on how this life is lived."

Stage Six. Like Sevens, Sixes spiritually march to the beat of their own drum: "Higher self resides inside of each of us. It connects us with our unique strengths, purpose, and principles, and with our commitment to reach our potential by pursuing these things." "Your spiritual self (or lack thereof) is heartfelt and chosen. It may even call upon you to connect with and feel love and awe for the beauty of nature and the world."

Stage Five. Spirituality (often in the form of the organized religion that is most familiar), as well as observing religious traditions, is an important part of life. However, the role of spirituality is often confusing and unsettled. In reflective moments, you ponder such questions as "What is the meaning of life?" or "Is this all there is?" as well as issues like the afterlife or God's role in tragedy and injustice.

Stage Four. "God is benevolent. If I do the right thing, God will love me."

Stage Three. Whether you are an atheist, a fundamentalist, or anything in between, there is a strict and inflexible set of rules to be followed not only by you, but by everyone else as well. "God is malevolent and unforgiving." "If I disobey God, I incur his wrath (burn in hell, etc.)." Religious dictums emphasize how followers are a different and better (or chosen) class of people than non-followers.

Stage Two. "There is no God. There are no consequences or rewards beyond the obvious ones, such as the justice system." "If you are not caught and punished, you have gotten away with something completely." "What you see is what you get."

Stage One. "'God' is whoever (or whatever) takes care of me."

Your spiritual beliefs can provide inner guidance for many aspects of your life. Many people consider their spiritual selves to be their most reliable source of truth. Practices such as prayer and meditation tend to open this channel wider and wider. In addition to the information in chapters 8 and 9, StageClimbing.com/resources will point you to many diverse views and sources of information to consider.

Families

How families operate at each stage:

Stage Seven. The family shares deep (often spiritual) values and is guided by both love and strong principles of service both inside and outside of the family or "tribe." Children are carefully and lovingly guided, by example and through experience, to be strong, respectful, empathetic, and highly decent individuals.

Stage Six. The whole is greater than the sum of its parts. The family is held together with love and respect. Family members support each other's passions, strengths, ambitions, and personal growth. They encourage one another to stay on the path to live their best lives.

Stage Five. When each member is functioning well in his or her family role, the family thrives. Problems occur when a member deviates from the family norm for a reason that is not clear to the other members. Examples: when siblings of similar ages are in different stages, or when children function at higher stages than their parents or other elders.

Stage Four. When these families are functioning well (generally headed by a benevolent matriarch or patriarch), family members validate one another. When the family is dysfunctional, self-esteem and self-confidence are weakened. Children who witness a lot of anxious behavior throughout their formative years are especially vulnerable to a variety of anxiety disorders. Approval and validation are often withheld as punishment.

Stage Three. The family is run rigidly by an authoritarian matriarch or patriarch. Stereotypical roles are unquestioned. Respect is demanded but not necessarily earned. Strict and sometimes severe punishment is mandated for failing to meet the often-stern expectations. Children go into the line of work and lifestyles that are expected of them more out of guilt, fear, and lack of reflection than by choice, often failing to consider other possibilities. Family members are sometimes ostracized or labeled as black sheep as punishment for not toeing the line or for failing to fit in.

Stage Two. Deception, anger, addiction, or abuse—which can be emotional, physical, or sexual—or extreme hedonism without regard for consequences are the staples of this highly dysfunctional family environment.

Stage One. Typically, family members are extremely enmeshed with each other and often feel unable to face the outside world with even a minimal degree of competence or independence.

When a family unit operates from Stages Six and Seven, it's obvious that every member benefits on a long-term basis. What changes—whether major ones or small tweaks—can bring different aspects of your family relations to those stages? Often the simple recognition of certain blind spots and alternatives to them can trigger a major breakthrough.

Love Relationships and Marriages

This calibration suggests that no matter where you are in your Stage Climbing process, there is a relationship for you. From which stage do you now operate? How about your partner? Use this calibration to discuss ways you can make your relationship work better through your support of each other. Also, clarify how you can make the climb together in order to optimize your relationship. This exercise could permanently raise the bar for both of you, as I have seen it do with many couples I have worked with.

If you are not currently in a marriage or love relationship, but are looking for one, be aware of what you are seeking in a prospective partner. Here is how partners typically relate to each other by the stages:

Stage Seven. The couple becomes a team who selflessly work together in a common mission beyond themselves, such as their children or their community. Each partner can easily put the other first, and one may even put the partner's mission above one's own without complaint or expecting a quid pro quo. Partners are beyond being attached to or governed by expectations.

Stage Six. Partners feel best about themselves and look to each other as a person to love and support as opposed to someone *from whom* love, sex, and validation are expected. There is genuine caring, intimacy, and respect that are not merely predicated on what each partner gets back. When Sixes tell their partners, "I love you," they mean just that.

Stage Five. Each partner dutifully fulfills the other's relationship slot and all that it entails, serving, for example, as sex partner, financial partner, companion, coparent, or best friend. Partners are not necessarily governed by passion or a strong attachment that transcends their roles.

Stage Four. Partners look to their relationship and to each other as a source of love, validation, and approval. The emphasis is on being loved (receiving) and validated as opposed to loving (giving). Fours often try to please their partners as a way of getting back as much or more affection. When they say, "I love you," it can mean, "I want you to love me." Fours may often ask their partners, "Do you love me?" and sometimes obsess about that. There is frequently an inordinate degree of jealousy and insecurity.

Stage Three. Both the foundation and the climate for the relationship are grounded in dictums— often clichés or stereotypes. These are usually based on long-standing rules and traditions governing such things as how partners meet; the religious or ethnic background of anyone who could be considered for involvement; who works and who stays home; the nature of sex life; fidelity; and beliefs about the need for permanency in love relationships and marriages. Disagreements often focus on who's most compliant with the rules that form the basis of the relationship. This "rule book" usually settles control issues and other conflicts as well.

Stage Two. Usually, one partner dominates the other or uses the relationship as a vehicle to act out in a variety of ways. Deception and even abuse is often the substitute for intimacy, One partner can demand that the other be faithful while he himself is not.

Stage One. The foundation of the relationship is principally security, dependency, and neediness (emotional or financial). Either or both partners may be preoccupied with "needing to be needed." A One is often experienced by his or her partner as a "bottomless pit."

In this important part of your life, what changes for you or you and your partner seem warranted?

Parenting from the Child's Point of View

A key to good parenting is to complement what is both age- and stage-appropriate. Consider this as a very basic guideline for ideal parenting *at each stage of the child.* (Note: the calibration in the next section addresses the stages of the *parents.*)

Stage Seven. You only need to feel proud and gratified for having been able to model and encourage Stage Seven behaviors. You as a parent have often put your own needs aside for those of your children without inducing guilt, and you have taught the values of service. To the extent that your children operate as Sevens, they have internalized those values. Respect from your children flows back to you synergistically.

Stage Six. By the time they reach this stage, hopefully you and your children are emotional equals. Obviously, however, you are still the parent. You are parenting your children as Sixes whenever you are enjoying the process of helping them grow in their own direction. (Sadly, parents in lower stages will often have difficulty understanding and appreciating their children in the two highest stages.)

Stage Five. You have a certain number of years to influence your children by example. By the time your children have reached Stage Five, chances are that whatever they have not already learned from you they will choose to learn elsewhere. So let go of any remaining need to control their lives. Allow and honor the right of your adult children to be independent and different from you. By doing that, you will command respect without having to demand it.

Stage Four. The goal here is to encourage self-exploration while carefully and lovingly setting limits, letting go and allowing your adolescent to make his or her own mistakes—all the while remaining a safety net and a source of love, support, and guidance. But it's also crucial to provide discipline and tough love whenever an adolescent child crosses the line. And those lines must be clear. This could be your last opportunity to be the principal source of influence for your child.

Stage Three. Here your goal is to provide a solid structure and to patiently teach the basic, yet complex, rules of life. These are your main challenges with Stage Three children. When you provide loving guidance along with appropriate discipline, children have the best possible environment to learn what it takes not only to fit in, but also to thrive and to begin to discover their own uniqueness through early Stage Six and Seven hooks.

Stage Two. To let the toddler explore, while teaching and setting limits and minding his or her physical safety, are the principal tasks here. Most important (and what is at times most difficult) is not to act out your own frustrations and emotions—especially anger—on your child. This period can be thought of as a trial run for adolescence, a stage that is a lot less demanding physically for the parent but can be much more demanding emotionally.

Stage One. Your aim is to provide unconditional love, nurturing, care, and safety during the child's first year of life.

Where have you noticed that this difficult balancing act called parenting could use a tweak?

Parenting from the Parent's Point of View

Now here is how parenting looks by the stages of the parents:

Stage Seven. Part of parenting your child from Stage Seven is to see that role as a calling, where putting your needs aside and sacrificing when necessary is done as a labor of love and purpose, not out of guilt or obligation. Many Sevens choose to become foster parents, adopt needy children, or serve in some mission involving children when they are unable to have their own, or when their own children are grown.

Stage Six. Those who parent from Stage Six will rarely miss an opportunity to learn more ways to be effective. Parenting is often seen as the most joyous, rewarding, and loving part of life. Observing each aspect of a child's growth can be a mesmerizing experience. Sixes both appreciate and encourage their children's uniqueness. They make genuine efforts to be mindfully present when interacting with their child.

Stage Five. Fives consider parenting their children to be another major role, albeit an extremely important and rewarding one.

Stage Four. Stage Four parents are often obsessed with being loved, respected, and considered a "friend" by their children.

Stage Three. While teaching rules and values are essential elements of parenting, Stage Three parents who rule their kids by fear and harsh discipline usually miss the mark. In this present era, parents (and others, such as teachers) have access to many resources and much information that they didn't have in past generations. Therefore any approach that puts the emphasis on fear and other types of harsh behavior may now be considered emotionally or physically abusive. *At best, these anachronistic measures don't translate to effective discipline.* Moreover, highly authoritarian Stage Three parents generally have difficulty with adolescents in particular, who may rebel to a dangerous degree on the one hand, or on the other hand become so fearful that they remain Threes both throughout and long after adolescence.

Stage Two. Stage Two parents may be neglectful or abusive emotionally, physically, morally, or even sexually for no reason that even pretends to benefit their children. In extreme cases, Twos have been known to use their children to beg, steal, deal drugs for them, or even worse.

Stage One. Parents who themselves operate as Ones—regardless of the child's age—may encourage their children to become "parentified," meaning the child acts in the role of the parent in one or more major ways, taking care of the parent emotionally and physically.

This calibration simply asks you to look at your own values and practices as a parent, and then ask yourself whether you are getting the result that you want.

Calibration Worksheet

Use this reproducible worksheet to make your own Stage Climbing calibration for any aspect of your life or issue you are working on:

Title: _____

Stage Seven

Stage Six

Stage Five

Stage Four

Stage Three

Stage Two

Stage One

The Basic Stage Climbing Drill

Identify a hook or an issue, or an area of your life in which you believe you are not functioning optimally:

_____

_____

_____

_____

Identify the stage from which you are currently operating with regard to the above issue, hook, or aspect of your life:

Stage 1_____ 2_____ 3_____ 4_____ 5_____ 6_____ 7_____

Choose your _target stage_. This is your goal or the stage from which you'd like to be operating with respect to this issue, hook, or part of your life:

Stage 1_____ 2_____ 3_____ 4_____ 5_____ 6_____ 7_____

Looking at this issue _through the lens of your target stage_, how do you now see it?

_____

_____

_____

_____

_____

_____

_____

By using both the calibrations in this chapter and any variations that you customize, identify the attitudes, beliefs, and behaviors that characterize your chosen target stage for this hook or part of your life.

To hardwire your new attitudes, beliefs, and behaviors, simply resolve to live by them. This will require some effort and practice until they become solid habits. New habits take an average of three to six weeks before they feel and become natural.

Sometimes that's all you need to do. In other situations, strategies from previous chapters may be needed to do this hardwiring. The appendix takes you through this drill in more detail for managing a problematic hook.

This Stage Climbing Drill is a resource that's always available to help you with any issue or challenge. Please use it often to you make your life exactly what you want it to be!

For additional help or to download these worksheets, visit www.StageClimbing.com/worksheets.

Appendix
The Stage Climbing Drill in Action
A Strategy for Managing Your Hooks
Across All Seven Stages

Here is a step-by-step strategy to help you use the principles of Stage Climbing in the most straightforward way to manage or remove a hook, and make the process work for you in the shortest time possible.

You can download the worksheet for this strategy at your convenience. Just visit www.StageClimbing.com/worksheets.

Breakthrough Strategy to Manage or Remove a Hook
Your hooks are your thoughts, feelings, or behaviors that are characteristic of stages other than how you normally operate in a given life area. To be fully in charge of your life, you need to manage your problematic hooks so that they do not become stifling hang-ups. This means to

identify and understand your hooks and bring them under your control. *Once you are able to manage your hooks, they simply represent more choices for you.* In other words, they go away when you don't want them, and they are available to you when you do. Each time you do this, you have taken another major step toward being fully and consciously in control of your life.

Please remember that the Stage Climbing process can only help you to make changes *within yourself.* This means changing an attitude, belief, or behavior that is driving a self-defeating pattern or negative emotion. *Changing another person or some set of circumstances outside of yourself is not an option* available to you with this exercise.

You may need to use additional paper to answer some of the questions below most fully.

To manage or remove a hook: identify the hook (or the issue related to one) that you would like to work on. Please choose only one hook to work on at a time:

_____

_____

_____

_____

_____

_____

_____

_____

Identify the stage or stages that typify the hook you are working on.

Below are the seven stages, along with a sampling of the most common attitudes and beliefs that would underlie a problematic hook at each stage (more versions of these appear in the chapters dedicated to each of the stages). Underline or highlight those that apply to you. In the space provided, fill in your customized version of the beliefs or attitudes at each stage that are powering your hook:

STAGE ONE HOOKS

- "I can't do it."
- "It's too hard."
- "I am inadequate."
- "I must be taken care of."
- "I am incapable of change."
- "I can't take the initiative to better my life."
- "I must be certain that a decision I make be the right one or I will not be able to decide (or handle the consequences)."
- "What's happened to me in the past (such as my childhood) makes it impossible for me to live a happy and fulfilling life now."
- "I am a powerless victim."

My version: _____

_____

_____

_____

STAGE TWO HOOKS

- "I must have and do whatever I want, regardless of the effect on anyone else."
- "I must have or do what I want regardless of the long-term consequences I cause to myself."
- "I don't want to change."
- "I will do or say whatever I have to in order to get what I want."
- "Life should be easy."
- "I must always be treated well, and anyone who doesn't is just asking for revenge."

My version: _____

_____

_____

_____

STAGE THREE HOOKS

- "I should or must or should not or must not (insert a rule that doesn't serve you, but you feel compelled to obey, even though you are not required to by any authority outside of yourself)_____."
- "I must fit in by doing only what I should do and by being what I should be."
- "I have to do what's expected of me, or something bad will happen."
- "Others should do things my way."
- "Others should believe what I believe."

My version: _____

_____

_____

_____

STAGE FOUR HOOKS

- "What other people think of me is crucial."
- "I can't stand it if I'm rejected by someone else. It's even a reason to reject myself."
- "I must be loved or approved of by others."
- "I have to meet other people's expectations."
- "I can only accept myself if I'm accepted by others."
- "I must do well at everything I do. Anything less than perfect is unacceptable."
- "Failing at something (e.g., a relationship, a job, an exam, a sexual performance, a goal) makes me a total failure."
- "_____ (fill in the name of someone specific) must love me just the way I want, or our relationship won't work."

My version: _____

_____

_____

_____

STAGE FIVE HOOKS

- "I can't handle (_____) in my life right now."
- "I'm overwhelmed."

- "I feel trapped with no way out."
- "I have to keep it all together."
- "I have to step up to the plate with my roles and obligations, even if they're not working for me."
- "I have it all, but I still feel unfulfilled."

My version: _____

_____

_____

_____

STAGE SIX HOOKS

- "I should feel personally gratified by everything I do."
- "Changing the world or helping someone else is not my problem right now."

My version: _____

_____

_____

_____

STAGE SEVEN HOOKS

- "I must save the world, or some part of it."
- "I must save a specific person."

Even though they might sometimes present minor conflicts, genuine hooks in Stage Seven will rarely be problematic for you once you identify them (unless they are lower-stage hooks in disguise).

My version: _____

_____

_____

_____

Now ask yourself these three questions:

Are any of the beliefs I have identified above and written down completely true?

     Yes_____ No_____

Does the attitude or belief behind this hook serve any purpose that would make me want to keep it?

     Yes_____ No_____

Am I open to adopting new attitudes or beliefs regarding this hook?

     Yes_____ No_____

If you answered no to the first two questions and yes to the third, write down how this hook and the attitudes and beliefs that underlie it might be affecting you. Note how things in your life would be different without these attitudes and beliefs, and if this hook were no longer problematic for you. (If you gave different answers to these questions, you may not be ready to tackle this particular issue, or you may need to keep working on it until you can arrive at these answers. This exercise is designed to get you there, but only if you are ready to pull out all the stops to make the shift.)

_____

_____

_____

_____

_____

_____

_____

_____

_____

_____

Hold on to what you've just written. *Refer to it whenever you need motivation in removing this hook.*

Next, use the list below as a selection of some new attitudes and beliefs that you can choose as healthy alternatives to the ones you have just identified (more versions of these appear in the chapters dedicated to each of the seven stages). Underline or highlight those that apply to your hook.

To the extent that you choose to live by the attitudes and beliefs below, your hook will no be longer problematic.

STAGE ONE

- "I can handle it and *I will*."
- "I'm tired of depending on others."
- "I will now begin taking charge of my own life."
- "There is no such thing as certainty, so I choose to be comfortable with uncertainty."
- "*Too hard* means *impossible*, which it isn't. What's difficult is merely a challenge I can handle."
- "I choose to be free of my past wherever it limits me."
- "I am no longer helpless."
- "I am not a victim anymore."

STAGE TWO

- "Being self-absorbed hasn't gotten me what I thought it would."
- "Nobody has *everything* they want."
- "I can't control how people treat me. I can only control my reaction to them."
- "Life is not always easy, and I choose to accept that."
- "There are long-term benefits *to me* in treating others as I would like to be treated."

STAGE THREE

- "I am ready to start examining the rules I've lived by."
- "I'm ready to start examining the rules that I have demanded that others live by."
- "I'm willing to be more flexible."

- "I'm willing to be open to new ideas that are now a better fit for me and my life."
- "Fitting in is only one of many choices that are available to me."
- "Other people have the same choices regarding how to live their lives as I do."

STAGE FOUR

- "People who won't accept me for who I am aren't worth my time or attention."
- "There is more to life than getting others to admire or approve of me."
- "Love and approval from certain people may be nice, but they're not essential."
- "I give myself unconditional acceptance regardless of who else does."
- "I can only do my best. I hereby let go of that impossible standard called perfection."
- "Failing at something does not make me a failure."
- "I can handle things even when I don't like them."
- "How anyone else feels about me is beyond my control."

STAGE FIVE

- "I want to be doing what I love."
- "I want to feel rewarded internally as well as externally for what I do."
- "I can handle being overwhelmed."

- "When I feel overwhelmed, I can use it to give me insight about deciding whether to take other things on."
- "Satisfaction is nice to have, but I accept that there are many things I choose to have in my life that don't provide it as much as I wish."
- "I now take responsibility for putting into my life that which will fulfill me."

STAGE SIX

- "Life is good, but there is more to life than my own gratification."
- "It's time to focus on the world that's larger than me."

STAGE SEVEN

- "On to the next mission!"

Using the above list for reference, write out new affirmations that represent how you choose to think and feel about this problematic hook. Make your list as comprehensive as possible. Use additional paper if necessary.

_____

_____

_____

_____

_____

_____

Now ask yourself these two questions:

Are my new affirmations regarding this hook *completely* true for me?

Yes_____   No_____

Do my new affirmations above remove or neutralize this hook?

Yes_____   No_____

If you answered yes to both questions, go to the next item below. Most importantly, commit yourself to living by your new affirmations. Refer to them as often as necessary until they become a hardwired part of you.

If, however, you answered no to either question, keep tweaking your affirmations until you can answer yes to both questions. If you are stuck, it will be helpful for you to revisit the chapter on the relevant stage.

Choose the *target stage* from which you would prefer to be operating whenever you are up against this hook. Consider this your goal.

Stage 1_____ 2_____ 3_____ 4_____ 5_____ 6_____ 7_____

When you look at this hook through the lens of your target stage, how do you see it? How is your attitude different? Is there anything else do you need to do, believe, or tell yourself so that you are never held back by this hook again? What other actions are you willing to take to move beyond it? Note your answers to these questions here. Refer to your affirmations and action steps whenever this hook challenges you again.

_____

_____

_____

_____

_____

_____

_____

_____

_____

_____

_____

_____

_____

_____

_____

In most situations, what you have done with this exercise is all you need to do. Of course you will also have to live by your newly chosen beliefs and attitudes regarding this hook. With your persistence, they will soon become second nature—a hardwired part of you.

Until your new attitude becomes natural and automatic, *act as if it is.* At the beginning, this may require some conscious effort. But you are simply walking the walk. This is the most powerful step to hardwiring new attitudes, beliefs, and affirmations.

Even if it is completely new to you, when you use this "act as if" technique, you are there as powerfully as if you had been there all your life. It will become as automatic for you as were the old attitudes and beliefs that powered your hook.

In case you're wondering why this is so, it's based on a simple principle of reinforcement. The higher stages tend to trigger an ongoing sense of internal fulfillment so that they are constantly reinforcing themselves. Thus they soon become an indelible part of you—much like any strong habits. That's your reward for your effort.

This strategy cannot fail as long as you are committed to staying with it until you achieve the results you want!

Epilogue
Embracing Your Seven Stages

To laugh often and much, to win the respect of intelligent people and the affection of children, to earn the appreciation of honest critiques and endure the betrayal of false friends, to appreciate beauty, to find the best in others . . . to leave the world a bit better, whether by a healthy child or a garden patch . . . to know that even one life has breathed easier because you have lived. This is to have succeeded!

—Ralph Waldo Emerson

I wrote this book with one principal intention: that you, my reader, will keep it close to you and refer to it often as new life challenges arise.

In addition, our website, StageClimbing.com—like life itself—is a work in process. We are constantly adding new strategies, calibrations, and other resources to help you optimize all aspects of your life. We will also continue to offer one-to-one and group coaching, online courses and seminars, blogs, articles, audios, videos, and new applications that you can use. So do stay in touch through StageClimbing.com, email, snail mail, our social media sites (become a fan on Facebook and follow us on Twitter), or by attending one of our events.

Please let us know how you are doing, how Stage Climbing has had an impact on your life, and how we can be of further help to you.

I hope that you will consider this not the end, but only the beginning of our relationship. Feel free to get in touch at any time that we can be of further help or support. I wish you much happiness, success, and fulfillment.

May you reach your highest potential in every part of your best life!

Michael S. Broder, Ph.D.

References

Broder, Michael. 1989. *The Art of Living Single.* New York: Avon.

———. 1993. *The Art of Staying Together*: New York: Avon.

———. 2002. *Can Your Relationship be Saved? How to Know Whether to Stay or Go.* New York: Impact Publishers.

Orwell, George. 1949. *Nineteen Eighty-Four.* New York: Harcourt, Brace.

Peck, M. Scott. 2003. *The Road Less Traveled: A New Psychology of Love, Traditional Values, and Spiritual Growth.* New York: Touchstone.

Index

About the Author

Michael S. Broder, Ph.D. is a psychologist, executive coach, continuing education seminar leader, popular speaker, and media personality. He is an acclaimed expert in cognitive behavioral therapy, specializing in high achievers and relationship issues.

Michael has appeared on *Oprah* and *The Today Show* as well as making over a thousand other radio and TV appearances. For many years, he hosted the radio program *Psychologically Speaking with Dr. Michael Broder*. He has been written about in *The New York Times*, *The Wall Street Journal*, *Time*, *Newsweek*, and hundreds of other publications.

His popular books include *The Art of Living Single*, *The Art of Staying Together*, and *Can Your Relationship Be Saved? How to Know Whether to Stay or Go*.

His many audio programs include *Positive Attitude Training, Self Actualization: Reaching Your Full Potential,* and *The Help Yourself Audiotherapy Series,* which is also used by mental-health professionals and coaches worldwide with their clients and patients.

Dr. Broder earned his Ph.D. at Temple University. He conducts seminars, talks, and presentations to professional as well as lay audiences worldwide.

For a more complete biography, please visit *DrMichael Broder.com/about*

Website: DrMichaelBroder.com

Email: MB@MichaelBroder.com

Phone: 215-545-7000 or 800-434-8255